DC VOTE

DC VOTE

▼

Fighting Against Taxation Without Representation

Edited by
Abdul Karim Bangura

Writers Club Press
San Jose New York Lincoln Shanghai

DC Vote
Fighting Against Taxation Without Representation

Writers Club Press
an imprint of iUniverse, Inc.

For information address:
iUniverse, Inc.
5220 S. 16th St., Suite 200
Lincoln, NE 68512
www.iuniverse.com

ISBN: 0-595-20912-2

Printed in the United States of America

To the Residents of Washington, DC!

CONTENTS

▼

CHAPTER 1

▼

INTRODUCTION

Abdul Karim Bangura

Introduction

This book is mainly about *what* DC Vote, The Coalition for DC Representation in Congress, does to fulfill its goal: to gain voting rights for the residents of Washington, DC in the United States Congress. Employing an interest group perspective, the book also examines *how* and *why* DC Vote engages in lobbying (i.e. attempts to influence policy makers) in the pursuit of its goal, and what have been its successes and shortcomings up to this point.

DC Vote is a formalized citizen aggregation or political interest group based in Washington, DC. This organization is mainly interested in determining the content and impact of various government policy decisions with respect to congressional representation for the citizens of the District of Columbia. Inevitably, the result of DC Vote's formation and activism is a preoccupation with all three branches of the federal government—executive, legislative, and judicial. Nonetheless, not a single, comprehensive work exists on the pursuits of DC Vote.

This is mainly because existing works on interest groups have focused primarily upon either the macro/national level (e.g., Mahood 2000) or the mezzo/state level (e.g., Rosenthal 1994). Since, due to their levels of analysis, these works are forced to examine many interest groups, they do not present a detailed account of the pursuits of any of the groups. Thus, the essence of this book hinges upon the fact that it provides a comprehensive, micro level analysis of the work of a single interest group, DC Vote. This is because, although science is concerned with the universal rather than the individual, sciences are constructed principally from, and should apply to, individual instances. This consideration suggests why empirical methods lend themselves to objectivity.

Overview

Established in 1790, Washington, DC is the capital of the most powerful nation on earth today. It comprises a population of more than half-million residents, none of whom have any voting representation in Congress. Like the United States territories—American Samoa, Guam, Puerto Rico, and the Virgin Islands, the District has a nonvoting delegate in the House of Representatives. But unlike these territories, the federal government does tax the District. Also, the residents of Washington, DC give more money to congressional candidates than the residents of any other city or state in the Union (http://www.dcvote.org). Yet, the money paid by the people of DC does not help support a candidate who can vote in Congress on behalf of these citizens; hence, the purpose of DC Vote. Its Web site clearly defines the organization's mission as an attempt

> to educate the public and the US Congress about the need
> for the citizens of the District of Columbia to enjoy full

voting representation in the US House of Representatives and US Senate. It brings together any and all organizations, citizens, and other supporters of the principles enumerated in the Constitution that guarantee democratic representation of all citizens and assert the principle of "one person, one vote" (http://www.dcvote.org).

To effectively fulfill this mission, DC Vote in September 2000 moved its offices from the downtown end of M Street, NW to the grassroots haven of U Street, NW. DC Vote is now located at 1500 U Street, NW, Washington, DC 20009. Occupying both upstairs offices and a storefront on the corner of 15th and U Streets, NW, the new space allows for better community access, more volunteer drop-in opportunities, and more room for administrative offices from which staff can manage DC Vote's growing local and national campaign efforts. Thus, the major question here is the following: What precipitated the emergence of DC Vote and its mission?

In Article 1, Section 8 of the United States Constitution, one reads:

> [Congress shall have the power] To exercise exclusive Legislation in all Cases whatsoever, over such District…as may, by Cession of particular States, and the Acceptance of Congress, become the Seat of the Government of the United States…."

Virtually since the birth of the Nation in 1776, there has been a debate over whether the seat of the national government or capital should have the same rights and privileges that are enjoyed by the States. The Framers of the Constitution did not believe that the capital should be another state. Instead, they sought to have a locale that was not within the purview and control of any other government.

Although, over time, there has been debate over the "right" of residents of the capital to voting power in the Congress, the fact still remains that more than two centuries later these citizens do not have congressional representation. Contrary to a bedrock of the Nation's creed,[1] defined in the Declaration of Independence, residents of Washington, DC do not enjoy taxation *with* representation. And although the residents of the Nation's capital are allowed to cast ballots for the highest office in the land—the presidency—and are allowed to levy and collect taxes, not to mention pay taxes to the national bankroll, these citizens are still not afforded representation in either house of the Congress.

While there exists literature on capitals throughout the world and throughout history that granted their residents representation in the supreme governments, the United States has remained steadfastly oblivious to the fact that Washington, DC, which could constitute one of the richest and most populace states in the Union, does not have a viable polity that may elect two Senators and representatives to the House of Representatives. Throughout its history, the District has had to receive special attention. For example, the landmark *Brown v Board of Education of Topeka Kansas* (1954), which outlawed discrimination in public schools and effectively dismantled racial discrimination in public accommodations, did not affect the Nation's capital because it applied only to "States."[2] Residents of the District had to sue the federal government, because the Supreme Court's decision was not legally being followed in the District. Since Washington, DC was not and is not a state, the 14th Amendment to the Constitution, which speaks directly to "state" action, did not apply to the non-state of Washington, DC. All these developments notwithstanding, residents of the District eventually won in the Courts a similar ruling. In *Bolling v Sharpe* (1954), the Supreme Court ruled that Washington, DC schools had to desegregate. The only difference here was that DC residents could not argue the 14th Amendment, but had to rely on the equal protection clause of the 5th Amendment to the Constitution.

In *Wesberry v Sanders* 1964, Justice Hugo Black writes:

> No right is more precious in a free country than that of hav-
> ing a voice in the election of those who make the laws under

which, as good citizens, we must live. Other rights, even the most basic, are illusory if the right to vote is undermined. Our constitution leaves no room for classification of people in a way that unnecessarily abridges that right.

The preceding excerpt is a true reflection of the voice that the District lacks in the American polity. Thus, the interest of DC Vote lies with the burden placed by the Constitution of the United States to ensure democracy: the right to vote. It is the right for District residents to have a say in the very government to which they pay taxes, labor in, and even defend in wars.

Historical Background

After declaring their independence from England in 1776, the American colonies began to set up their government. When the Founders reviewed the Articles of Confederation in 1787, they decided to establish a capital district under the control of the federal government. This decision resulted in part because of an incident that occurred earlier in Philadelphia while the Continental Congress was in session. A group of Pennsylvanian veterans lodged a peaceful protest outside Independence Hall to demand payment for their service in the Revolutionary War (1775-1783). The Congress asked the Pennsylvania State council to address the situation, provide protection, and break up the protest, but the council did nothing. The legislators adjourned and reconvened in Princeton, New Jersey, only after coming to the conclusion that the affront to their power would not have happened had there been a permanent seat of government under the exclusive control of Congress (Green 1967:10). The decision of where to locate this new seat of government was a huge debate and vote.

This was just the beginning of the DC voting issue. Some in Congress felt that the location for the new capital should be located "centrally." This became a contentious issue because they could not decide if centrality should be based on geography or population. Finally, in a caucus, a decision was made. The North agreed to the location being in the South, in exchange for the South assuming the debts of the Revolutionary War. Thus, The Residence Act of 1790 was passed. President George Washington chose the land near the Potomac River from parcels of land belonging to Maryland and Virginia.

When Congress took control and moved into its new seat of government in 1800, it realized that it had not discussed the political status of the citizens of the new capital. These citizens formally of Washington and Alexandria Counties and the cities of Washington, Georgetown and Alexandria were without a governmental structure. George Washington appointed three commissioners to govern the city (the same commissioners who had been hired to build the capital). The President also appointed marshals and justices of the peace, as well as established levy courts made up of officials from outside the city limits to assess taxes and manage local affairs. Under the same legislation, Congress established a circuit court and stated that District residents did not have the right to vote in national elections or have representation in Congress.

Within the District of Columbia, the cities of Georgetown and Alexandria continued to govern themselves under their own established charters. In 1802, Congress approved a charter to establish a government for the city of Washington within the District. The charter included provisions for the following: (a) a mayor appointed by the President; (b) the mayor to appoint all the officers; (c) a twelve-member council elected by the voters with the authority to pass laws and impose taxes; (d) the council could override the mayor's veto by a three-fourths vote.

Congress made changes to the original charter throughout the next 20 years that affected the city's government structure. These changes were as follows: (1) In 1804, the charter was amended to give additional powers to the city council. This included "...the power to prohibit gambling, to superintend the health of the city,...to provide for the establishment and superintendence of public schools" (Furer 1975:66). (2) In 1812, in the second charter of Washington, the city council was expanded to twenty members and given the power to elect the mayor. (3) In 1820, voters were given the right to elect the mayor.

In this structure, the citizens still did not have much power over the affairs of their government. The decisions made in these charters were those of members of Congress, individuals who had no affiliation with the very area for which they were deciding policy. Even with a city council and a mayor, Congress still maintained full control over the District.

After the Civil War (1861-1865), the businessmen of the District asked Congress to take a more active role in the local affairs of the area. The businessmen believed that this would increase revenue to the region. They also feared that the increasing influence of the African American vote would undermine the region. The population of the District after the war was 131,700, with an African American population of 43,422. So, with the influence of these business leaders, Congress passed the District Territorial Act which became law in 1871. The Act provided the following: (a) the abolishment of existing city and county governments (Georgetown, Washington City, and Washington County); (b) a governor, an 11-member council (the upper house of the legislature), and a Board of Public Works, all appointed by the President; (c) the governor to approve all legislation; his veto could be overridden by a two-third vote in both houses of the legislature; (d) congressional authority to repeal or modify all legislative acts; (e) a 22-member House of Delegates (the lower house of the legislature) elected by the voters; (f) a non-voting delegate to the House of Representatives elected by the voters; (g) the legislative assembly to reach a two-third vote to borrow money; (h) the legislative assembly to tax residents and non-residents at the same rate; (i) the legislative assembly to provide public schools; (j) the legislative assembly to appoint justices of the peace and legislate concerning the acts of the courts (United States Congress House Committee on the District of Columbia, 101st Congress, 2nd Session, 1990:42).

These changes motivated by the wealthy and their prejudice once again took away from the prospect for a self-government in the District. Again, the upper echelon of the District government was appointed and regulated by the president and the Congress. These were the same president and congressmen for whom District residents could not vote. The only advantage of the District Territorial Act for the District's residents was that it did allow them to vote for a delegate to the House of Representatives. Although the delegate was a non-voting member, the Act was a move towards giving DC residents a presence in Congress.

Nonetheless, the District Territorial Act was short-lived. The Organic Act of 1878 removed the existing government and replaced it with a three-person commission, comprising two civilians and an officer of the Army Corps of Engineers. The Organic Act did not allow for city council representation, and it removed the non-voting delegate to the House of Representatives. This form of government existed until the mid-1960s.

While the commission form of government existed, the 23rd Amendment to the Constitution was passed in 1961. This amendment allowed the citizens of the District to vote in presidential elections for the first time. It also established three Electoral College votes for Washington, DC. At this point, President Lyndon B. Johnson began to push Congress to pass some form of home rule for the District. From 1949 to 1973, any efforts to pass any form of home rule was blocked by the Chairman of the House Committee on the District of Columbia.

The chairmen of the committee during this period were members from southern states. Between the 1950s and the 1960s, members from both the House and Senate introduced some form of bill for the District of Columbia's Home Rule. The Senate did pass four home rule bills. However, these bills failed because they were not allowed to leave the House Committee on the District of Columbia. This was largely due to the opposition of the committee's chairman, John L. McMillan (Democrat-South Carolina), and its eight southern members.

In 1967, Johnson took it upon himself to introduce the Reorganization Plan Number 3. Even with opposition, mainly from Republicans and southern Democrats, the plan was passed. The new plan was to abolish the three-member Board of Commissioners. It would establish a commissioner, a deputy commissioner, and a nine-member council to be appointed by the President. The commissioner and council would assume legislative and executive powers.

This move by Johnson was to hopefully transform the District government into one resembling home rule. By the 1960s, Washington, DC's population was majority African American. So, the commissioner and council were to resemble the District's makeup. The President appointed a majority of African American officials who could be elected once a home rule bid was successful.

The 1973 home rule bill passed by the Senate represented the eighth time since 1949 that this body had approved a bill providing some measure of self-government for the Nation's capital. The Senate's bill was much stronger than the House's version, with differences finally being resolved in conference. Based on the original House and Senate bills, it seemed that the District was on the verge of gaining the desired control over its own affairs. For many reasons, however, this cherished goal eluded the District once again. Although rarely mentioned, underlying the arguments on home rule and its different facets were the issues of race and politics. The fact that the population of the District was predominantly African American and heavily Democratic left many Republican and southern members of Congress either lukewarm or opposed to a popularly elected local government (Harris 1995:7).

Finally, the Home Rule Act was passed by Congress, signed by President Richard Milhouse Nixon, and ratified by the District's residents by a vote of 83,530 to 18,037. The act allowed for the following: (a) a mayor to be elected by District residents; (b) a 13-member council elected by District residents; (c) eight-members from each of the eight wards of the city; (d) four at-large members (no party can nominate more than three candidates); (e) a chairman of the council; (f) the court system to remain as the District of Columbia Court Reform and Criminal Procedure Act of 1970 had established.

This was a major step towards what the District had been attempting to achieve for nearly 200 years. Another advance to the representation of District citizens was the reinstatement of the non-voting delegate to the United States House of Representatives. The Reverend Walter E. Fauntroy filled this office. Fauntroy, a native of the Shaw area in the District, received his divinity degree from Yale University and returned to the area to serve as minister to the New Bethel Baptist Church. His theme was and continues to be "revitalization for the District."

In 1975, the citizens of the District elected their first mayor, Walter Washington, who had served as the commissioner of the city. Sterling Tucker was elected as the first chairman of the city council. The District still lacked the representation it desired in federal legislation. The new government and statehood and civil rights advocates continued to push for more representation and a voice in the federal government, the very government that still maintained discretionary control over them.

In 1978, Congress passed the DC Voting Rights Amendment. It would have amended the Constitution to treat the District as if it were a State for the purpose of federal representation, by creating two voting United States Senators and one voting Representative. However, it failed after being ratified by only 16 states within the seven-year period provided for ratification. Thirty-eight states were required for approval.

In 1979, DC voters approved the Statehood initiative. Pursuant to that act, DC voters elected their first Shadow Congressional Delegation in 1990. On September 21, 1993, the House of Representatives took a vote on the people's petition for statehood for New Columbia. Despite support from President William Jefferson Clinton and other high ranking Democrats for statehood, HR 51 was rejected by a vote of 277 to 153. The denial of representation in Congress does not only lock District residents out of the national legislature, it also locks them out of a state legislature. Thus, Americans living in the District are the only citizens of the United States today who have voting representation neither in Congress nor in a "State" legislative sovereignty.

Despite the bid for New Columbia, the District still enjoyed the luxury of the limited home rule it had. In the second election after the Home Rule Act was passed, Walter Washington lost his bid for reelection as mayor to Marion Barry in 1978. Barry's election was a result of the District citizens exercising their right to vote for a candidate they chose to represent them. Barry gained his recognition with citizens through his activism. He was a founder of the Student Non-Violent Coordination Committee, home rule advocate, and former member of the District's School Board.

While in office, Barry tackled many issues that reflected his platforms and views of the District's residents. Many times, Barry was at odds with the city council, as well as the House Committee on the District of Columbia. Despite the opposition of the House Committee, Barry continued to fight for the plight of the District's residents—the very people who exercised their long awaited right to vote for a person to represent them. Barry's commitment and drive to speak for his constituents afforded him three consecutive terms as mayor.

In 1990, Sharon Pratt Dixon replaced Barry as mayor. Her tenure was not like that of Barry. She encountered stiff opposition in terms of stabilizing the financial crisis of the city. She claimed that the financial crisis was created by Barry's administration. Dixon, whose name changed in office to Sharon Pratt Kelly, was not able to solve the city's budget deficit.

In 1994, Kelly lost her bid for reelection to the very person she blamed for the city's turmoil, Marion Barry. He had returned from his conviction to be elected to the city council as the Ward 8 Council Member. From there, he sought the mayorship. In achieving this, Barry won his fourth term as mayor.

During Barry's first year as mayor in his fourth term, critics chipped away at his credibility. Congress slowly stripped many of the powers of the mayor. The fiscal management of the city was turned over to the DC Financial Responsibility and Management Assistance Authority, better known as the DC Control Board. Its function was to review the city's operations and budgets and put mechanisms in place to turn it around by the new millennium.

In a seemingly ironic twist, after Barry announced that he would not be seeking reelection, the Control Board announced that the new mayor would regain the powers of government on a gradual basis. He then endorsed a new candidate for mayor, Anthony Williams, the very person who was hired by the Control Board to serve as the Chief Financial Officer for the District. In his position, Williams was responsible for the cutting of the District's budget, not to mention District jobs. Williams managed to win over long-time DC political icons such as Kevin Chavous and Harold Brazil. Williams was victorious in the General Election, defeating Republican challenger Carol Schwartz. This election placed the instruments of powers back with the people, albeit "restricted" powers.

In sum, the District of Columbia is the last American "colony." Ironically, it was the very status America fought against to create its own sovereign government.

Basic Organization of the Rest of the Book

The rest of the book is divided into five chapters, an epilogue, and a commentary. Each chapter begins with an introduction of the topic being discussed. It then proceeds to examine existing perspectives and relevant findings on DC Vote about the topic. In the end, a conclusion is drawn.

Chapter 2 by Lisa Nicole Nealy discusses the political economy of interest groups. The focus of this chapter is on group politics, interest group formation, and economic incentives for group membership.

Chapter 3 by Patrick D. Nemons examines the interests of DC Vote. In this chapter, attention is paid to the type of interests DC Vote promulgates.

Chapter 4 by Carol J. Roberts is about funding for the activities of DC Vote. More specifically, it looks at the methods employed by the organization to raise financial resources to support its efforts.

Chapter 5 by Damon Lamont Waters presents techniques used by DC Vote to lobby policy makers. The major emphasis here is on *how* the organization goes about gaining *access* and *persuading* policy makers.

Chapter 6 by Kathy Booh is about *who* are being targeted by DC Vote in the pursuit of its agenda. Discussed in this chapter are the policy makers and branches of government that have been the targets of DC Vote, and how these individuals and government entities have responded.

In the epilogue by Ray M. Crawford, Jr. an assessment is made about the prospects for Washington, DC representation in the United States Congress. Here, the views and activities of both supporters and opponents of DC voting rights in Congress are taken into consideration.

Finally, five separate commentaries by Martin Thomas, Mark Plotkin, John-John Williams IV and Karen Richards, *The Washington Post*, and Julianne Malveaux, respectively, are presented. The essence of these essays is why and how Washington, DC residents must fight to gain equality.

Endnotes

1. In the Declaration of Independence, the authors state the following as one of the reasons for the quest of their freedom: "For imposing Taxes on us without our Consent," which has been historically interpreted to signify the lack of governmental representation selected by the people that participated in the creation, levying and collection of taxes. The Colonists charged that King George taxed them without their due consent, which made this act unjust and contrary to the laws of nature.

2. *Brown v Board of Education's* application denied States the authority to deny equal access to education based on the Equal Protection Clause of the 14th Amendment of the Constitution. This amendment ordered that all citizens born or naturalized in the United States should have due process of and have equal protection under the laws.

CHAPTER 2

▼

THE POLITICAL ECONOMY OF INTEREST GROUPS

Lisa Nicole Nealy

Introduction

This chapter is concerned with the *Political Economy of Interests Groups.* *Political Economy* is defined as selective goods or incentives available only to those who participate in the group. Selective incentives can be tangible or intangible. A tangible incentive or benefit can be a hospitalization plan, an insurance policy, or a subscription to a professional journal (Mahood 2000: 19). An intangible benefit can be satisfaction gained from interacting with like-minded persons or feelings of satisfaction gained in working toward the goals of a group. Thus, the benefits derived or obtained from group formation is considered the *political economy* of an interest group. Cost, time and effort can also be viewed as characteristics of the *political economy* of an interest group. Indeed, there are specific problems that emerge from this *political economy* of group formation. The problem of collective incentives gives rise to a *"free-rider"* dilemma. When an individual joins a group but fails to put forth an effort in achieving a common goal of the group, she/ he will still benefit from the efforts of other group members. Stated differently, *free-riders* are those individuals who join a group just to receive benefits without any cost being attached.

Therefore, the purpose of this chapter is twofold. First, it provides the reader with several theories concerning the political economy of interest groups proffered by Arthur Bentley, David Truman, Earl Latham, Robert Salisbury, E.E. Schattschneider, Theodore Lowi, Mancur Olson, Carole Pateman, Dennis Chong, and Douglass Heckathorn. Second, it analyzes how DC Vote fits within the theoretical frameworks explicated by these group theorists regarding the *political economy of interest groups*. This is salient because DC Vote has a genuine national interest in achieving full citizenship for all Washington DC residents.

Perspectives on Political Economy of Interest Groups

Theories regarding the political economy of interests groups emerged in 1908. The earliest discussion on political interest groups in the twentieth century commenced with the leading pluralist named Arthur Bentley, who illuminates his views in *The Process of Government (1908)*. In this work, Bentley presents a theoretical framework of interests groups based on *conflict theory.* This theory assumes that public policies emanate from competing interest groups. Bentley argues that interests groups were more pervasive than political institutions (Bentley 1908:210). He also believes that *group* interests were more salient than *individual* interests.

Truman's views concerning interest groups are similar to Bentley's arguments regarding the notion that group interests are more important than individual interests. Truman's theoretical framework is based on *disturbance theory,* which assumes that socioeconomic disturbances lead to group formation. Truman's framework offers a more empirically based rationale for Bentley's thesis (Mahood 2000: 14). In his important work entitled *Governmental Process* (1951), Truman argues that, when the existence of the political status quo is threatened (i.e. wars, immigration, changes in economic forces), new groups emerge. According to Truman, these transformations of the group universe occurs in waves, such as what occurred in the civil rights and environmental movements of the 1960s. The number and existence of groups in a society, according to Truman, serve as an index of stability within a society, and their members may be used as an index of their complexity. In this light, Truman proposes an idealized version of the democratic nature of political interest groups. This would produce various alliances and coalitions of interests that represent the public good.

Latham is another pluralist who perceives politics to be influenced by the existence and political activism of many political interest groups. Latham's theoretical framework is based on an exclusive *group theory* of interest group formation. In his article entitled "The Group Basis of Politics" (1952), Latham delineates the structural components of how groups organize and present themselves as *structures* of powers. He avers that such groups are seen as structures of power because they concentrate their energy in achieving a purposeful goal (Latham 1952: 376-7). Latham links this structural component to the *state* as being a social system of the individual. For instance, Latham indicates that the state must compete with conflicting group loyalties because most people think of themselves first as members of their clubs, lodges, unions, or parishes, and only incidentally as members of the state (1952:366-7). Latham also recognizes that the state and other group forms represent power in different packages, and that organized groups may be regarded as systems of private government while the organs of the state represent a system of public goods (1952: 352).

Salisbury is another pluralist who views group formation as essential to specific organizations. His theoretical framework is prefaced on the *exchange theory* of interest groups. This theory suggests that interest group origins, growth, death, and associated lobbying activity may all be better explained if one regards them as exchange relationships between entrepreneurs/organizers who invest capital in a set of benefits, which they offer to prospective members at a price-membership (Salisbury 1970: 33). In his book, *Interests Group Politics In America* (1970), Salisbury offers an extensive examination of how exchange theory focuses on the development of American agricultural groups. In his analysis, Salisbury introduces the *proliferation* and *homeostatic mechanism hypotheses* to determine how American agricultural groups come into being and the conditions affecting their growth or decline.

The *proliferation hypothesis* proposes that, as a consequence of various processes of social differentation, especially those linked to technological change but include others as well, there is within a given population more and more specialization of function (Salisbury 1970: 33-34). For example, Salisbury maintains that American farmers became increasingly specialized in terms of the commodities raised in a particular area or by particular farmers. The *proliferation hypothesis* suggests that, as a natural social response among conflicting specialized groups, formal associations are created, or emerge, to represent the conflicting claims of each differentiated set of interested parties. Thus, it is the association which articulates the interest, and, by organizing its adherents, provides more effective bargaining power vis-a-vis other groups (Salisbury 1970: 35).

Conversely, the *homeostatic mechanism hypothesis* places less emphasis on the processes of social differentation and the generation of new interests. It assumes a certain differentation and suggests the following sequence as typical of group origin. A putative equilibrium among social groups is disturbed as a consequence of such social disruptive factors as technological innovation, war, transportation or communication changes, and such macro-social processes as major population movements, business cycle fluctuations and industrialization (Salisbury 1970: 35). Salisbury observes that a disequilibrium will evoke response from the disadvantaged sectors, as they seek to restore a viable balance (1970: 36). Therefore, this hypothesis implies a cyclical pattern of membership that would be expected to rise in conditions of adversity, and probably decline or at least stabilize when adversity is overcome (Salisbury 1970:39).

Furthermore, there are vociferous arguments made against the pluralist school of thought for advocating the notion of *group* interests rather than focusing on the *individual* who lacks the ability to *organize*. Anti-pluralists such as Schattschneider, Lowi, Olson, and Pateman have criticized the pluralist notion concerning a democratic process which excludes certain groups from organizing. In his classic books entitled *Party Government (1942)* and the *Semi-Sovereign People* (1981), Schattschneider addresses these issues of political parties and the people being the actual *sovereign* of their interests. In doing so, he presents a theoretical framework that is premised on a *party government* theory of interest groups. This theory assumes that political parties are unique custodians of democracy which do a better job in representing the interests of the majority instead of a few. In other words, Schattschneider is arguing that interest groups are inadequate to represent the interests of the majority.

Schattschneider further argues that political parties are mere aggregators of interests. He points out that the majority of Americans do not have any interest group representation, which is the major flaw with the pluralist paradigm (Schattschneider 1942). Schattschneider recognizes class bias associated with belonging to interests groups. For example, those individuals who are rich join political interest groups to strengthen democracy, but the poor are excluded from this democratic process (Schattschneider 1981).

Lowi's view of interest groups is parallel to Schattschneider's arguments. In his book entitled *The End of Liberalism* (1979), Lowi maintains that interest groups are self-serving rather than serving the interests of the general public. He formulates his theoretical framework based on this very idea of *interest group liberalism* that assumes interest groups are less susceptible to bargaining, which creates resistance to change. In this vein, democratic government ceases to function as the Founding Fathers intended. He indicates that the *people* are shut out of the national agenda setting and policymaking by entrenched private interests, namely interest groups (Lowi 1979).

Olson also concurs with Schattschneider and Lowi regarding the pluralist notion of interest groups. While Schattschneider and Lowi highly criticize the theories of Bentley, Truman, and Latham regarding interest groups, Olson attacks the empirical analysis of these pluralists. An economist, Olson maintains that Truman fails to present a logical empirical theory of interest groups (Olson 1965). Hence, Olson formulates an empirical theory that diametrically opposes Truman's theory of interest groups. In his famous work, *The Logic of Collective Action: Public Goods and the Theory of Groups* (1965), Olson postulates a theoretical framework premised on a *rational-choice* theory of interest groups. This theory assumes that individuals are rational when they do not support groups' goals over their own goals. Specifically, Olson is critical of the idea that interest groups organize whenever there is a reason to do so. He draws a distinction between *actual* groups and *latent* groups, seeing the latter as the most critical. Olson argues that, the *actual* groups, when they are fortunate enough to have an independent source of selective incentives, will organize to achieve their objectives (Olson 1965).

In addition, Pateman's theoretical framework centers on a *theory of participatory democracy* of the individual. This theory assumes that one learns to participate by participating. Simply, only the minority participates where pluralism masks a hidden conservative agenda (Mahood 2000: 18). In her book, *Participation and Democratic Theory* (1970*)*, Pateman elucidates this theory of participation by asserting that individuals and their institutions cannot be considered in isolation from one another. In illustration, the existence of representative institutions at rational levels is not sufficient for democracy; for maximum participation by all the people at that level of socialization, or social training, democracy must take place through the process of participatory democracy (Pateman 1970: 42). She indicates that in order for a democratic polity to exist, it is necessary for a participating society to exist, i.e. a society where all political institutions have been democratized and socialization through participation can take place in all areas (1970: 42). Hence, Pateman concludes that individuals should organize so that they can influence decision-making (1970: 43).

There have been recent theories regarding the *political economy of interest groups* offered by offsprings of the pluralist camp. These offsprings are Chong and Heckathorn, who write about the collective action problem of interest groups. Chong focuses on the collective action problem of social movements, whereas Heckathorn's emphasis is on social dilemmas of collective action. Both Chong and Heckathorn's theoretical framework is closely linked to Olson's framework of interest groups. In his book, *Collective Action and the Civil Rights Movement* (1991), Chong presents a theoretical framework which centers on the *dynamics* of *public-spirited collective action*. This theory assumes that collective outcomes become an end for the group. He defines *public-spirited collective actions* as large scale political activism that is motivated by public concerns such as the environment, peace, civil rights, women rights, and other moral and ideological issues (Chong 1991: 1).

According to Chong, public-spirited collective action is characterized by a situation in which potential activists will participate if they are confident that other activists will also participate to make their efforts worthwhile. An example of a public-spirited collective action is the civil rights movement, which seeks radical changes within the American ethos. Chong suggests that the civil rights movement represents a populace of potential activists who become organized for protest which requires the development, mobilization, and association of an organized group. Steadfast leadership within the movement is crucial for the initiation of collective action to be translated into collective outcomes. However, Chong also argues that this public-spirited collective action of an interest group creates a problem called *prisoner-dilemma*. This occurs when a member makes choices to go along with decisions made for the entire group or simply become a defect. Heckathorn's framework examines this defect problem.

Heckathorn's theoretical framework is premised on a *reductionist theory* of interest groups. This theory assumes that voluntarism, cooperation, and strategic interaction are key components in eliminating the prisoner dilemma faced by interest groups. In his article, "The Dynamics and Dilemmas of Collective Action" (1996), Heckathorn argues that collective action proceeds from initiation to rapid expansion to stability, its game type organized in a way that can be precisely characterized as movement through a two-dimensional game. Heckathorn describes two ways of promoting collective action: (1) resolving the dilemma within a particular game, and (2) changing the game of the dilemma to be easily resolved or eliminated (Heckathorn 1996: 253). Heckathorn then suggests that, without voluntarism, cooperative and strategic interaction with each member of the group, collective interests will fail to produce any kind of collective action. He also notes that all oppressed groups revolt, even when the power vastly exceeds that of their controllers.

Collective action includes two distinct levels. The first level refers to personal contributions to produce the collective good. In the simplest case, individuals have the choice of contributing (cooperating at the first level) or not contributing (defecting at the first level). One may decide whether to participate in a demonstration or help build a new canoe for one's village. The second level refers to what are termed *second-ordered collective goods* such as selective incentives to reward first level cooperation or punish first level defectors (Heckathorn 1996: 214). Heckathorn's model suggests that individuals are assumed to make different choices at the first level and make trichotomous choices at the second level. At the first level, individuals make a choice whether to contribute to collective goods produced at cost i.e. the cost of cooperation at level one. The amount each actor can potentially contribute is assumed to be equal to those by others. At the second level, actors are assumed to have three choices: (1) they can contribute to a selective incentive system at cost two, or the cost of cooperation at level two; (2) they can oppose the system of selective incentives at cost two, the cost of opposition at level two; (3) they can defect at this level, incurring no costs (Heckathorn 1996: 253-4).

How does DC Vote fit within the aforementioned theoretical frameworks of the *political economy of interest groups*? To answer this question, one must first discuss this organization's mission. The mission of the Coalition for DC Representation in Congress is to educate the public and the Congress of the United States about the need for citizens of the District of Columbia to enjoy full voting representation in the U.S. House of Representatives and the U.S. Senate (http://www. dcvote.org).

Findings on DC Vote

DC Vote's strategies are similar to those suggested in the general literature on the *political economy of interest groups*. For instance, the pluralist school of thought, led by Bentley, Truman, Latham, and Salisbury argue that *group interests* are more important than *individual interests*. Simply, group formation is key to achieving a desired outcome. In this light, DC Vote is and can be aligned with the pluralist school of thought regarding interest groups. Amy Slemmer, the executive director of DC Vote, agreed to a face-to-face interview in which a multiplicity of queries were asked concerning the *political economy* of this interest group. Slemmer's responses clearly parallel the views held by Bentley, Truman, Latham, and Salisbury regarding interest group formation.

According to Slemmer, DC Vote is a non-profit national organization which organizes across the state to achieve national interests. DC Vote is organized in Washington, DC to achieve tangible benefits which include congressional voting representation for the citizens of the District of Columbia (personal interview with Slemmer on October 23, 2000). Slemmer states that every person of voting age will have full representation in the United States House of Representatives and Senate where a total of three electoral college members would be rendered, i.e. one vote in the House and two in the Senate. Slemmer also alludes to some of the intangible benefits DC Vote hopes to achieve are to convey a positive message to the children in the District that they can aspire or reach their fullest potential by pursuing elected public office (personal interview with Slemmer on October 23, 2000).

Further, Slemmer addresses the *collective action* and *free-rider* problems within DC Vote. She avers that, if a collection action problem occurs, it is dealt with by forming a consensus among members of the organization. She also indicates that since DC Vote is a fairly young organization, a free-rider problem hasn't manifested yet because each member brings his/her own talents to the table. Slemmer also discusses the socio-economic backgrounds of DC Vote members. She suggests that their socio-economic backgrounds vary as represented in the District. In other words, *all* people in the District of Columbia are represented by DC Vote.

Moreover, the anti-pluralist school of thought maintains that interest groups are only concerned with *individual interests* rather than *group interest*. Lowi suggests that interests groups are *self-serving* rather than serving the interests of the general public. Contrary to Lowi's views, DC Vote is concerned with *group interest* exclusively. For example, Slemmer notes that DC Vote is fighting for the rights of every Washington, DC citizen. She also points out that most people should try to understand the *individual* personal stories of the people in the District whose plight is to gain suffrage.

DC Vote proposes at least four ways that the citizens of DC can achieve full and unified voting representation in Congress: (1) *Washington, DC Statehood*—the U.S. Congress has the authority to admit new states into the Union under Article IV, Section 3 of the Constitution. If Washington, DC was made a state, it would be entitled to two seats in the U.S. House of Representatives. DC residents would then have a state government, which would replace the current form of local government and carry all the rights and responsibilities of a state in the Republic. (2) *Direct Statutory Enfranchisement*—Congress currently treats Washington, DC as a state for over 500 different purposes. Congress could pass a law providing Washington, DC with two US Senate seats and the appropriate number of US House seats based on its population. While stopping conferring statehood on Washington, DC under such a law, voting representation in both the US House of Representatives and the Senate would be added to the list of purposes for which DC is treated as a state. (3) *Retrocession to*

Maryland—the area that now makes up Washington, DC was once part of the state of Maryland. For a period after the federal government took control of the land from Maryland and Virginia, citizens living in DC continued to vote for, and even run as, congressional candidates from those states. With the consent of Maryland's state legislature, the non-federal portion of DC could similarly be returned to Maryland, giving citizens in DC the right to vote in local, state, and federal elections as residents of Maryland. Under this scenario, the current city of Washington, DC might become a city or county in the state of Maryland (http://www. dcvote.org).

Although DC Vote has not been successful in achieving the aforementioned goals, Slemmer enunciates that the organization's mission to influence public policy by lobbying Congress to give DC citizens full representation is still obtainable. Irrespective of Congress' failed efforts to endorse DC Vote's policy, Slemmer argues that other organizations have embraced it. However, as Olson maintains, interest groups organize whenever there is a reason to do so. He argues that there is a dichotomy between *actual groups* and *latent groups* whenever they form. In illustration, Olson indicates that *actual groups* will organize to achieve their objectives when they have an independent source of selective incentives (Olson 1965*)*. These views expressed by Olson run parallel to the views held by Slemmer regarding DC Vote objective in organizing. Slemmer indicates that there would be no need for DC Vote if DC residents had voting rights. Given this aim, Slemmer correctly classifies DC VOTE as an *actual group* whose primary reason of organizing is to win the battle of DC voting rights for all DC citizens. In this light, Slemmer argues that the organization's goal is to put itself out of business (personal interview with Slemmet on October 23, 2000).

Needless to say, Chong and Heckathorn, who represent the new generation of group theorist argue that interest groups are underscored by *public spirited collective action* and *prisoner-dilemma*. Chong suggests that public spirited collective action entails large scale political activism that is motivated by public concerns such as moral and ideological issues (1991:1).

He also avers that strong leadership within interest groups depends on whether or not their collective outcomes are achieved. According to Slemmer, DC Vote is absolutely a *public-spirited group* who has been tenaciously involved in large scale activism at the national and local levels (personal interview with Slemmer on October 23, 2000). She further notes that strong leadership within DC Vote does influence whether the organization's collective outcomes are obtained. She points out how other talented individuals within DC Vote cooperate or work together to get the job done.

Even more, Heckathorn argues that interest groups are confronted with a problem known as *prisoner-dilemma*. To paraphrase Heckathorn, prisoner-dilemma occurs when a member chooses to go along with decisions made for the entire group or simply defect. To remedy this defect, voluntarism, cooperation and strategic interaction are key in resolving a prisoner dilemma (Heckathorn 1996: 253). According to Slemmer, DC Vote has not been faced with a situation of prisoner-dilemma, but anticipate it occurring in the future. She indicates that, if this problem occurs, some members will get people to join the organization or simply leave. Most of the members are volunteers who became actively involved with DC Vote by cooperating and vigorously supporting the organization's strategic agenda in gaining full representation for DC residents. Slemmer also suggests that those members who choose to stay in the organization are rewarded by highlighting them in the organization's monthly newsletter and receiving personal gratitude from the board of directors (personal interview with Slemmer on October 23, 2000).

Slemmer further that DC Vote is affected if some members choose to terminate their membership because it will lose other organizations endorsements. She adds that DC Vote's endorsement comes from other interest groups such as Common Cause, League of Women Voters, and Civil Rights Organizations whose financial support is vital to the organization's survival. Slemmer states that the total number of members in DC Vote ranges from more than fifty endorsing organizations commingled with thousands of individual signatures on their petition. Lastly, Slemmer indicates that there is no fee charged for joining DC Vote; however, she plans to implement changes by January 2001 for all members to begin paying dues (personal interview with Slemmer on October 23, 2000).

Conclusion

Given the aims and goals of DC Vote, this interest group fits within Chong's theoretical framework of *public-spirited collective action*. First, DC Vote is an organization which seeks radical change through nonviolent measures in achieving a common cause for DC residents—enfranchisement. Second, DC Vote is a large group whose members represent the interests of a large majority of DC residents. Third, DC Vote has a large scale political activism that is motivated by one essential public concern—full citizenship for DC residents. Although DC Vote is not a social movement, it is a political organization that has galvanized the community of DC in supporting its primary mission.

Finally, despite the gallant efforts of DC Vote's struggle to gain political representation for DC residents, it has not achieved any true *tangible collective outcomes*. The organization has only produced *intangible incentives* for DC residents such as shadow representation in Congress, where delegate Eleanor Holmes serves as the voice for DC residents. Many DC residents are somewhat satisfied with having a shadow representative in Congress who articulates the desire interests of the majority of DC residents for enfranchisement. Thus, the tangible incentives being full citizenship for DC residents represents the end goal of DC Vote which has yet to materialize.

CHAPTER 3

▼

INTERESTS

Patrick D. Nemons

Introduction

The major interest of DC Vote lies within every individual, whether in America or abroad, who has a desire to participate in a democratic society. This chapter is about the interests of those residents and other individuals who seek representation for the District of Columbia in local and federal affairs that directly affect them. As already stated several times in this book, due to the current state of affairs in the District's electoral process, it lacks voting rights in the United States Congress. Furthermore, the individuals District residents are allowed to elect are governed by the very body in which they have no vote.

The ultimate purpose of this chapter is to examine the interests of DC Vote, as articulated by citizens and proponents, as well as past and present leaders. This will help to describe the attempt to seek the simplest rights enjoyed by all Americans, i.e. the right to govern and take part in their own affairs.

The rest of this chapter covers existing perspectives on the interests of interest groups, the interests of the DC Vote, and an analysis of those interests. The core information is derived from DC Vote, other groups pursuing District voting rights, and secondary sources on interest groups in general.

Perspectives on Group Interests

To fully comprehend DC Vote's interests, it is important to examine a sample of the available literature on interest groups to delineate the general nature of group interests. Interest groups have been very effective in getting problems to government or getting issues on what political scientists call the "institutional agenda." Of course, groups such as the American Medical Association (AMA) and the National Rifle Association (NRA), which command considerable financial and organizational resources, have more success in tilting public policies in their favor than the resource-starved and poorly-organized groups.

Interest groups in America, as Graham (1990:3) observes, provide an alternative form of political participation to voting or membership in a political party and may, in certain respects, provide a superior form of participation. Interest groups help in raising issues that are too detailed or specialized to be the concern of political parties or central in election campaigns. Thus, interest groups allow intense minorities: that is, groups vitally affected by a policy issue to prevail over majorities to whom the issue matters little.

Berry (1989:6) lists the roles played by interest groups as: (1) to represent their constituents before government; (2) to afford people the opportunity to participate in the political process; (3) to educate the American public about political issues; (4) to get involved in agenda building, which basically turns problems into issues that become part of the body of policy questions that government feels it must deal with (institutional agenda); (5) to monitor programs to make sure that they deliver to their constituents what they were intended to deliver, and that program implementation is in compliance with the law.

Participation in American interest group politics increased significantly in the 1980s, as these groups continued to replace political parties as the dominant organizations of American politics. Hrebenar and Scott (1990) describe this sharp decline of political parties and the related rise of interest groups as articulators of political demands as the "era of new politics."

There are many terms used to denote organizations that are involved in lobbying to affect public policy decisions. Such terms as "pressure groups" and "special interest groups" have acquired a negative connotation because they are viewed as self-serving and not concerned about public interest at large. The term "interest group," though not devoid of this negative connotation, is seen as somewhat neutral and will be used interchangeably with the term "lobby group" in this chapter.

An interest group can be said to be engaging in *lobbying*, if it attempts to influence policy makers. Actually, the word lobby comes from the practice of interest group representatives standing in the lobbies of legislatures so that they could stop members on their way to a session for a quick discussion of the merits or demerits of a bill.

Truman (1971:33) defines an interest group as any group that is based on one or more shared attitudes and makes certain claims upon other groups or organizations in the society. Making those claims upon other groups or organizations involves lobbying.

Lobbying can be used as a technique for gaining legislative support or other institutional approval for a given objective. The objective could be a policy shift, a judicial ruling, or the modification or passage of a law. Mahood (1990:53) points that lobbying is also employed to reinforce support for established policies or it can be used to activate allies for defensive purposes, especially to oppose a policy shift and maintain the political status quo.

Hrebenar and Scott (1990:2) use the 1987 Judge Robert Bork confirmation hearings to show how lobby groups can affect policy decisions in America. More than 185 liberal organizations opposed Judge Bork. Among the notable organizations were Norman Lear's People for the American Way (PAW), the AFL-CIO, the National Organization of Women (NOW), the National Abortion Rights Action League (NAAL), the National Association for the Advancement of Colored People (NAACP) Legal Defense and Educational Fund.

Judge Bork's conservative support was quite strong and included such groups as the American Conservative Union (ACU), Concerned Women for America (CWA), the National Rights to Work Committee (NRWC) and such influential television evangelists as Reverend Jerry Falwell of the Moral Majority, Dr. Robert Grant of the Christian Voice, and Pat Robertson of the 700 Club. The liberal interest groups waged a skillful fight to defeat the nomination. Actually, the loss in the full Senate by a record vote of 58 to 42 was an impressive victory credited to the liberal interest groups.

The liberal interest groups' victory should be balanced with the 1991 nomination of Judge Clarence Thomas to the Supreme Court against much opposition from some of the same liberal interest groups. Judge Thomas' confirmation by the Senate by one of the narrowest margins in history (52-48) was much more involved than the Bork nomination because women as a group played a significant role in pressuring their senators to vote against Judge Thomas. Such senators as Joseph I. Liebermann of Connecticut, Richard H. Bryan and Harry Reid of Nevada, who had been solid supporters of the Judge during the hearings, ended up voting "No." They were joined by three other Democrats who initially had hinted that they supported Judge Thomas—Bob Graham of Florida, Daniel Patrick Moynihan of New York, and Robert C. Byrd of West Virginia (*The New York Times* October 16, 1991).

So, even though it was a victory for the conservatives, it was a narrow victory that could have gone the other way had three more senators caved in under pressure and voted against Judge Thomas. That case would have given the liberals yet another victory. The Judges Bork and Thomas hearings are just two examples of how different lobby groups can get intensely involved in an issue or nomination that they feel could affect their members, favorably or unfavorably. Lobbying in Washington is big business, and all sectors of the economy are represented. Big business has numerous representatives in Washington, but most businesses and corporations also belong to such umbrella groups as the powerful National Association of Manufacturers (NAM) and the United States Chamber of Commerce (USCC). The USCC, founded in 1912 to be the major voice for business interests in America, is the largest and best known group in America. The Chamber grew out of the insecurity which pervaded the business world in the period immediately preceding World War I. Businesses saw themselves threatened not only by labor, but also by the federal government. Instances of such presumably hostile attitudes were the passage of the Sherman and Clayton (Antitrust) Acts, the vigorous prosecution of trusts (large corporations controlling certain industries) by the Theodore Roosevelt Administration, and the growing demands of disadvantaged groups for increased regulation of business (Ziegler and Peak 1972:229).

Business groups recognize that government action, whether in the form of economic policy, monetary policy, or regulatory policy, directly affects their performance in the market and the economy at large. Thus, they will actively lobby to influence such government policies in their favor. Hrebenar and Scott (1990:263) cite the 1977 lobbying effort by the American Telephone and Telegraphy Company (AT&T) for passage of a communications bill that would discourage competition in the telephone business, to show how big businesses can aggressively push their cases in Congress to tilt the legislative scale in their favor. AT&T in this endeavor beefed up its push for the bill with expenditures of over $2.5 million during the 1976-1977 legislative year.

Organized labor has been a major lobbying force in American politics since the mid 1950s, when the AFL and CIO merged into a powerful labor union (AFL-CIO) and lobby, representing millions of skilled and unskilled workers. Labor continues to invest heavily in candidates deemed to be "friendly to workers." Even though labor's endorsed candidates in the 1980 and 1984 presidential elections were not elected, an AFL-CIO endorsement still carries much weight and is well sought after. Most of the work involved in getting political influence is done by the AFL-CIO's political arm, COPE (Committee on Political Education), which spends millions of dollars in each election year on contributions to candidates, registration drives, encouraging voters to vote and educating them on political issues deemed crucial by labor.

Farmers, who make up about two percent (2%) of the nation's population, are represented by a large number of agricultural groups. But the two major farm lobbies are the American Farm Bureau (AFB), which represents the wealthy, and the National Farmers Union (NFU), which represents the lower income farmer. AFB favors a limited economic role for government, whereas NFU favors government intervention and support for farm products. The professional organizations are also well represented in Washington. Two of the most influential groups in this category are the American Medical Association (AMA) and the National Education Association (NEA). These two groups launched very intensive lobbying campaigns especially in the recent presidential election years (1992, 1996, 2000) during which a number of issues of concern to these two groups were at stake.

One of the issues that is currently at stake is the national health policy which is going through a reformulation stage. AMA is opposed to compulsory national health insurance and hospital control legislation and intensively lobbies against such legislation. The AMA leads all other individual interest groups in money given to elected officials and often heads the list in the distribution of political money in elections. The AMA led the donations list with $1.4 million in contributions in 1974, increased to $1.7 million in 1976, and a first-place contribution of $1.6 million to congressional and senatorial candidates in 1978 (Hrebenar and Scott 1990:276). The AMA's intensity as a lobby group to influence the national health policy can be demonstrated by its strong campaign against Medicare. It reported spending between $7 million and $12 million in 1962 to fight Medicare (Dekin 1966:222).

In addition to professional associations, there are religious groups, ethnic groups, racial groups, pro-or anti-abortion groups, veterans associations, gay and lesbian groups, and feminist groups. The list of those represented is long and includes even welfare recipients who are represented by the National Welfare Rights Organization (NWRO), which was formed in the 1960s to lobby for increased federal welfare programs.

Ornstein and Elder (1978:29) argue that ethnic cultural groups such as AHEPA (the Greek American cultural association), the Italian American Foundation (IAF), and the Polish American Congress (PAC), as well as groups like B'nai B'rith, the Knights of Columbus, and the National Association for the Advancement of Colored People (NAACP) serve in part to reinforce their members' identification with ethnic, religious, or racial backgrounds. It is important to note, however, that emphasis of these ethnic cultural groups has shifted to lobbying for or against issues that affect their members. For example, rather than focus on ethnic iden-tification, NAACP lobbies for such issues as civil rights and increased funding for inner cities which are important for its members. The American-Israel Public Affairs Committee (AIPAC) also falls under this category; but the emphasis of its activities has been lobbying for the State of Israel, which its Jewish members consider a top priority issue.

Lobbying, as can be seen, has become an important vehicle for getting problems to government and for influencing public policy. Lobbying is not limited only to organized domestic groups. Individual citizens are known to lobby Congress for passage or defeat of legislation that they consider important to their interests. For example, Texas billionaire and former presidential candidate, Ross Perot, hired a lobbyist to influence Congress to enact an amendment to the Internal Revenue Code that would have had the effect of reducing Perot's tax liability (US Congress 1977:97).

Foreign governments are also well represented in Washington. Ornstein and Elder state the following:

> Virtually every foreign nation of significant size has a lobbying agent or agents operating in Washington. Many foreign agents are prominent political figures. They lobby Congress and the State Department on such diverse issues as military aid, most-favored-nation trade status, and allowing the concord supersonic airplane to land and take off in the United States (1978:51).

Representation by a lobbyist is considered crucial because lobbyists can gain access to key policy makers and win their confidence. They are knowledgeable and have the requisite bargaining and technical skills. They have the ability and the skills to put their client's case on the front burner. In the words of Edward Rollins, former White House Aide to President Reagan and Co-Chairman to the Ross Perot failed presidential campaign, "I've got many, many friends who are all through the agencies and equally important, I don't have many enemies...I tell my clients I can get your case moved to the top of the pile" (*National Journal* 1986:1052).

The next section of this chapter focuses on the specific interests of DC Vote. The major purpose is to see which of the interests discussed in this section are similar to those of DC Vote.

Findings on DC Vote

Since *The Residence Act of 1790* that established the District of Columbia, there has always been an interest in the vote for its citizens. Many of the perspectives of earlier years have maintained their momentum in current time. The perspectives have not been those of a whole group or individuals of like minds, as many have been of bipartisan opinion. Many established groups sharing the DC Vote interests have been formed to address the concerns and issues.

The first major act since 1790 was the 23rd Amendment to the United States Constitution, passed in 1961, which provided citizens of the District to vote in presidential elections for the first time. This was important because the amendment also established three Electoral College votes. Now, for the first time, the vote of the District was recognized, at least in the selection of the President of the United States. The citizens still did not have a similar recognition in the House or Senate, which was not satisfactory to them or their supporters.

Bipartisan interests were expressed to the Congress. The Republican President Richard Nixon expressed the sentiment that "It should offend the democratic sense of this nation that the citizens of its Capital…have no voice in Congress." The Democrat President Jimmy Carter stated that "There should be no doubt that District residents deserve full voting representation." In the Senate, Democrat Robert Byrd of West Virginia noted that "The people of the District…suffered more lives lost in the Vietnam War than 10 states…conscription without representation." A Republican view in the Senate came from Robert Dole of Kansas when he opined that "The Republican party supported DC voting representation because it was just, and in justice we could do nothing else."

These views from the presidential and senatorial levels of government express the interest of those working the political machine from within. Regardless of this verbal support, no concrete action took place in the executive and legislative branches to make it a reality. When the Home Rule Bill was passed in 1973, it represented the eighth time since 1949 that the Senate had approved a bill providing some measure of self-government for the Nation's Capital. But still, it provided no votes in Congress for the District.

If no actions were taken to make the liberation of the District a reality, then what was the talk of support about? One would suspect that the talk of Johnson and Nixon was the interests of politicians attempting to secure votes. As of 1961, the District had three electoral votes up for grabs. As for the Senators Byrd and Dole's input, it could have been in their best interests to bow to the pressure of the citizens of America, their constituencies, or securing votes for their tentative presidential campaign. Was there any sense of sincerity in the hearts and minds of those individuals? The answer to this question only laid in the minds of those individuals.

Still dissatisfied, without the full voting package, District citizens continued to fight and lobby. They had all the characteristics that defined an "interest group," according to the outline of Berry (1989:6) discussed earlier. The citizens (1) wanted their position heard before government; (2) wanted the opportunity to participate in the political process; (3) wanted the American public to be aware of the rights denied them; (4) wanted to make the issue of "Taxation Without Representation" part of the institutional agenda; and (5) wanted to monitor programs in place, such as the committees on the District, and to make sure that they deliver to them what they rightfully deserve and to motivate change for independence.

The existing interests are those of the average citizen, some sincere politicians, and some interest groups. DC Delegate, Congresswoman Eleanor Holmes Norton, has repeatedly expressed the view that, unlike the residents of the territories, District residents pay $1.9 billion annually in federal income taxes, making them third per capita among the 50 states and the District of Columbia. Thus, DC residents are the only Americans who must comply with every obligation without enjoying every benefit of citizenship. They have fought and died in every war since the American Revolution. In the last war, Desert Storm, DC sent more participants per capita than 47 states.

The current interests, like those of prior years, have enjoyed bipartisanship support. Congresswoman Norton received support in September 2000 when she met with the House Rules Committee. She was joined by DC Subcommittee Chairman Tom Davis and Vice Chairwoman Connie Morella to request a return of the delegate's vote. The Rules Committee of the 106th Congress has still not ruled on the request. The reason for not acting on the request is really unknown. It would be unfair to say that the reason is partisan because the Chairman and Vice Chairwoman are both

Republicans. It also would be unfair to say it is racial because, again, both the Chairman and Vice Chairwoman are White.

Of the interest groups concerned with the District of Columbia voting issues are The Coalition for DC Representation in Congress Education Fund (DC Vote) and Common Cause. The interest of DC Vote is, as stated earlier, to educate the public and the Congress of the United States about the need for citizens of the District of Columbia to enjoy full voting representation in the U.S. House of Representatives and U.S. Senate. The Coalition brings together any and all organizations, citizens, and other supporters of the principles enumerated in the Constitution that guarantee democratic representation of all citizens and assert the principle of "one person one vote." The Coalition is open to all who whish to pursue those goals through nonviolent means and with respect for all other members of the Coalition (www://dcvote.org).

Common Cause, an affiliate of DC Vote, is a collectivity of citizens who care deeply about their democracy. Common Cause is dedicated to playing a leadership role in the effort. Between these two interest groups, the objective is clearly obvious. They both want the District of Columbia to VOTE in Congress. Although District citizens can vote for their local government and the delegate they send to only one house of Congress, their vote does not ultimately matter. The legislation discussed and voted on by elected officials are subjected to final vote by the very body in which the citizens have no voting right.

Conclusion

Why won't Congress give the District the right of representation? The question cannot be easily answered. It is hard to tell what is in the minds of those individuals in the position to do so. Is it that the issue is racial because of the large population of African-Americans in the District? Is it because big business will be affected? Is it because it will create another Democratic Party state and Democratic votes in Congress? One thing is certain: one can only speculate about the main reason.

When groups such a DC Vote interact with lawmakers to express the concerns of the District citizens, they are doing so in the interest of all citizens. In some cases, as in the Ross Perot situation, individuals may lobby on their own behalf. In such a situation, it becomes not only what one knows, but also who s/he knows. Through these many attempts and political maneuvers, the existing perspectives of the interests of the DC Vote have not really changed from those since 1790. One can give citizens of a territory self-government and a position in the body. But, what does it all mean when the citizens ultimately have no say in their own interests? What does it matter when the citizens die for and pay taxes to a government that does not acknowledge its interests? The interests of the citizens are not satisfied when they are merely pacified with a facsimile of input in its own affairs.

CHAPTER 4

▼

FUNDING

Carol J. Roberts

Introduction

The effort to secure full voting representation in Congress for the citizens of the District of Columbia will require a sustained education and action program. If the citizens of the District of Columbia expect to have any success in achieving full and unified voting representation in congress, DC Vote must raise vast amounts of money. The primary fundraisers of this organization must have the ability to articulate their goals. These fundraisers must also possess the ability to focus on minute details.

This chapter discusses the funding initiatives of DC Vote. Funding is the process by which money is raised to support the programs of the organization. Next, the focus is centered on the techniques used by this organization to raise necessary funding. Finally, this chapter explores other techniques that might be applied to this organization's efforts to raise funds. This is important because, by utilizing different techniques, it increases the possibility of DC Vote achieving its fundraising goals.

Methods of Fundraising

The need to raise millions of dollars for political campaigns, especially for costly television advertising, has stimulated the development of many new fundraising techniques. Campaign financing has moved beyond the small, face-to-face circle of contributing friends, supporters and partisans (Dye 2000).

There are numerous methods used to solicit funds. Corporate, foundation and government grants are some of the most important sources of funding. Contributions are sought through a variety of solicitations, which are targeted toward individual citizens, such as direct mass mailing, raffles, phone-a-thons, and the sale of merchandise. Finally, celebrities have also become a major force in fundraising.

The philanthropic marketplace in the United States is colossal. In 1990, there were over 450,000 nonprofit organizations (other than religious congregations) in this country entitled by the Internal Revenue Service (IRS) to solicit tax exempt funds. Because of the caring and generosity of millions of American citizens, philanthropy is a major part of this nation's way of life. Successful fundraising efforts use carefully learned and tested techniques (Edles 1993).

Corporate, foundation and government grants are major fundraising sources. A grant is the giving of funds for a specific purpose. As long as there are needs and interests that require funding, there will be a demand for grants. And as long as there are wealthy individuals and profitable companies looking for ways to impart their values and demonstrate their concerns, as well as governments willing to fund research and efforts to find new and better solutions to social problems, there will be grantseekers (Bauer 1999).

In 1997, for example, corporations and foundations awarded over $21.6 billion in grants, while the government awarded approximately $90 billion. Most grantseekers believe that corporate and foundation giving is about equal to the federal government's. They are surprised, even shocked, to learn the truth. The amount of federal money awarded is more than four times the amount of private money awarded, which is one of the reasons why it is always a good practice to check out federal funds first (Bauer 1999).

An example of this is that sometimes the federal government itself becomes the sponsor of an interest group. It may give a contract or grant to an interest group (even to one attacking it), or it may pay the expenses of a group that wants to testify before an agency. The latter kind of support is called "intervenor funding." For instance, when the Federal Trade Commission (FTC) was considering rules that would restrict television advertising aimed at children, it paid about $77,000 to Action for Children's Television (Act), a group favoring such rules, so that it could gather and present information (Wilson 1983).

Political action committees (PACs) are groups whose main aim is to financially promote the political goals of particular interest groups. Rather than seeking large donations from a small number of very wealthy individuals, these groups raise small amounts of money from large number of contributors and combine them for maximum effectiveness (Berman and Murphy 1999). Approximately 4,000 PACs that vary both in size and structure exist today. The greatest number of PACs is generally aligned with business interests. More than 40 percent of all PACs today are associated with corporations. Labor unions, once a major source of campaign contributions, now rank third (Mahood 2000).

The 1996 elections are a high-water mark in terms of the amount of soft money (contributions by national parties to state parties to encourage greater voter participation through voter registration, party building, and get-out-the-vote drives) raised and spent by both major parties (Mahood 2000). Some $263.5 million in soft money was raised and spent in 1995-1996 to influence various electoral out-comes across the nation (Daly and Keen 1997).

PACs are probably the primary source of cynicism and distrust of politics in the United States today. Many journalists, reformers and even some
politicians are highly skeptical of PACs, and voters, increasingly frustrated
with a system of campaign financing heavily dependent of the money of
special interests, hold Congress in lower and lower esteem each year. The
problem, according to journalist Brooks Jackson, "isn't corruption; it is
more serious than that." He contends that "money can twist the behavior
of ordinary legislators. The system of money-based elections and lobbying
rewards those who cater to well-funded interest,…and it also punishes
those who challenge the status quo" (Jackson 1990:87).

New technologies have increased the reach and effectiveness of interest
groups. One of these new technologies is computerized and targeted mass
mailing (Godwin 1988). For many decades, interest groups have been
sending out huge mailings to people whose names are on lists culled from
telephone directories and other sources. Some of these mailing are sent out
indiscriminately. Mass mailing is used by all kinds of interest groups, but it
has been especially refined by public interest groups, which are sometimes
accused of being a small headquarters with a good mailing list. Today's
technology can produce personalized letters targeted to specific groups,
called targeted direct mail. Targeted letters are an excellent method to raise
money from people who share a common concern (Burns et al. 1997).

Common Cause is perhaps the best example of a public interest group
that successfully uses mass mailings. This organization promotes campaign
reform, the abolition of political action committees, and the elimination
of unneeded bureaucratic institutions. Common Cause has more than
250,000 members and an $11 million annual budget (Wilson 1983). Its
central target has been the abuse of money in the political process
(Rothenberg 1992).

Selling raffle tickets is another means of raising funds. It is necessary to
check with local law enforcement agencies to determine whether raffles are
legal in a community. Some groups have called raffles "a special prize program" to circumvent legal programs in areas where raffles are not permitted.

High ticket items (such as cars) make it possible to sell a limited number of tickets at a higher price (Edles 1993).

Phone-a-thons can be done successfully to raise funds. A room with desks and phones is all that is needed. If the space is lent to the organization, the profits should be greater because the expenses should be lower. To make the operation successful, volunteers are needed to make calls during the day and evening (Freedman and Feldman 1988).

The role of celebrities as interest group fundraisers is increasing. An efficient fundraising device is to have a popular personality (actor, musical performer, sports or a political figure) appear at functions such as benefits, concerts, dinners, golf or tennis tournaments. Admission fees can be charged. The cost of admission to the event depends on the popularity of the celebrity. When enough tickets are sold, the profits are usually impressive.

The key to a successful celebrity fundraising activity is the ability to find a popular personality who is willing to appear free or at a reasonable price. The funds from this activity can be boosted by holding a "meet the celebrity reception" following the event (Freedman and Feldman 1988).

Fundraising Methods Employed by DC Vote

DC Vote has a unique ensemble of fundraising methods. Foundation support and corporate sponsorship play a major role in its fundraising efforts. House parties and utilizing the support of well-know celebrities are other methods employed by this organization to raise funds. Finally, selling merchandise, door-to-door canvassing of neighborhoods, and solicitation of funds through piggy-back fundraising and electronic means are also methods used by DC Vote to raise funds. The following foundations are major contributors of DC Vote fundraising efforts.

The Arca Foundation, which is the leader among local foundations supporting education about the disenfranchisement of DC residents, gave a grant of $85,000 recently to the Coalition for DC Representation Education Fund to support litigation and organization efforts to win equal representation in the United States Congress for District of Columbia citizens, and to send law students into District of Columbia public schools to educate students about the issue (*www.folner.org/grantmaker*).

The Shefa Fund, an independent organization located in Philadelphia, Pennsylvania, provided a general support grant to DC Vote. This fund is a public foundation that conducts programs for the Jewish community about social responsibility; makes grants, advises Jewish funders, conducts workshops and consults with Jewish institutions (http://www.jrs.org/jir/8c0nnjy).

The Tides Foundation is a public foundation dedicated to progressive social change through creative philanthropy. With over 250 donor-advised funds, the foundation supports local, national and international organizations in the area of social and economic justice and the environment. In the past 20 years, the foundation has awarded over $100 million in grants and 1998 grants reached almost $20 million. The foundation also provides management services to other philanthropic organizations (http://www.folner.org/grantmaker).

The Naomi and Nehemiah Coher Foundation located in Washington, DC and Israel is a solid supporter of DC Vote. (*http://www.jirs.org/jirs/8c0nyry.htm*). It also has provided significant, but undisclosed, funding to DC Vote.

The Meyer Foundation was started in 1944 by Eugene Meyer, an owner and publisher of *The Washington Post*, and his wife, Anges E. Meyer. The Meyer Foundation is one of the Washington area's oldest private grantmaking foundations. It awarded over $8 million in 2000 to area nonprofit organizations (*www.meyerfoundation.org/info*).

Dynamic Marketing Concepts Web Design located in Washington, DC is a corporate sponsor of DC Vote's Web page. One of the other services this company provides is direct mailing.

The DC Vote provides detailed information on how to plan a successful house party. The host of the party is provided with a house party kit, which includes:

(1) phone call record sheet
(2) sign-in sheet

(3) pledge and volunteer sheet
(4) 100 invitations
(5) It's Time Video
(6) 25 DC Vote information packets
(7) 25 buttons
(8) 25 bumper stickers
(9) 1 yard sign

The house party is one of the most successful fundraising activities of DC Vote. It is also successful because persons on almost any economic level can give a party. The purpose of the party is to bring prospective donors together to listen to a presentation about the goals of the organization. After light refreshments are served, donations are requested.

Concerts, dinners and other fundraising activities where celebrities are involved raise considerable amounts of money. Jack Kemp, former HUD Secretary and Republican Congressman, was the featured speaker at DC Vote's first fundraiser. The co-hosts of the affair were Senator Edward Kennedy and Dr. Dorothy Height, the chairperson of the National Council of Negro Women. The event was a great success and brought out many one-time and new supporters (*www.dcvote.org/January.htm*).

Another example of a fundraising activity is the reception that was held at Georgia Brown's restaurant. It drew a large group of Washington's political leaders, including Congresswoman Eleanor Holmes Norton and council members David Catania, Carol Schwartz, Phil Mendelson, Charlene Drew Jarvis, and Harold Brazil. Mayor Anthony Williams pledged to raise one million dollars for the campaign to achieve full representation in Congress for the citizens of the District of Columbia during his opening remarks at a welcome reception for DC Vote's new executive director, Amy Whitcomb Slemmer (*www.dcvote.org/ octnov.htm*).

Taxation Without Representation merchandise is being sold by DC Vote to raise funds. License plate holders, tee-shirts, keychains, baseball caps and the five-minute educational videos are being offered for sale. The purchasing forms are found on the DC Vote Web page (*http://www.dcvote.org*).

Door-to-door canvassing of neighborhoods serve many purposes. First of all, it gives the canvasser the opportunity to explain the goals of DC Vote. If this is the neighborhood where one resides, it affords one the opportunity to exchange pleasantries with his/her neighbors. In addition to meeting neighbors, canvassing gives one the opportunity to select individuals for his/her next house party. It also gives one the opportunity to display some of the merchandise being sold by DC Vote. Finally, it provides one with the opportunity to solicit donations.

DC Vote joined in the seasonal flurry of election-year fundraising in the District by piggybacking on the parties and mailing done on behalf of congressional candidates who represent other Americans. Some 2,000 DC Vote return envelopes were distributed to activists, from across the political spectrum, who included them in their candidate fundraising. "This is a unique effort," stated Joseph Sternlieb, President of DC Vote. "We are launching it in order to both raise money for our national education campaign and to let all members of Congress know that their own contributors also support equal representation in Congress for all Americans" (*www.dcvote.org/funding.htm*).

DC Vote has an excellent Web page. One of the sections requests donations. These donations can be made online with a credit card or through the mail. The mailing address is provided.

On November 14, 2000, I had an enlightening conversation with Ms.Amy Whitcomb Slemmer, the executive director of DC Vote. Ms. Slemmer is also in charge of fundraising activities for DC Vote. She repeated the mantra that DC Vote is both a local and national educational program designed to educate the public on its purpose, which is to secure full voting rights for the residents of the District of Columbia. Ms. Slemmer reiterated that millions of dollars will be needed to achieve the organization's goal.

Conclusion

Educating the residents of the District of Columbia, the surrounding communities and the nation in regards to the goal of DC Vote, which is achieving full voter representation for the citizens of the district of Columbia in Congress, requires continuous and effective efforts. Thus, DC Vote will continue to require major support from private, corporate and foundation sponsors. House parties and utilizing the support of well known celebrities and dignitaries must continue to play a major role in the fund raising efforts of DC Vote. Selling merchandise, door-to-door canvassing of neighborhoods, solicitation of funds through piggyback fundraising and electronic means must also continue to be an important part of DC Vote's fundraising efforts. Indeed, millions of dollars are needed for the educational and action programs in order for this organization to achieve its goal.

CHAPTER 5

▼

TECHNIQUES OF INFLUENCE

Damon Lamont Waters

Introduction

Over time, DC residents have utilized various techniques to gain representation in the United States Congress and receive equal treatment as the fifty states. Overall, the law, in particular the Constitution, has had to be reinterpreted to apply to the District because of its peculiar nature. The District is not a state and most of the Constitution either allows or decries state action. This chapter delves into the techniques utilized by District residents to circumvent that peculiar nature through DC Vote to gain full representation in the Congress.

The chapter discusses the techniques adopted by DC Vote, from letter writing campaigns, to bumper sticker distribution, to direct governmental lobbying and litigation. The law, arguably, is not on the side of DC Vote;

this notwithstanding, attempts have been made and quite creative campaigns have been waged to garner local and national support for DC voting authority. The chapter looks at the specific activities of interest groups seeking redress from the federal government, but with an emphasis paid to DC Vote and its efforts to get the residents of the District beyond a non-voting delegate to achieve representatives correctly enumerated based on its citizen population and two voting Senators.

Interest groups have become the primary link between citizens and their government. As a channel of access through which people can present their views to public officials, interest groups afford people an efficient and effective opportunity to take part in the political process. Since American political culture stresses that participation is a virtue and apathy a vice, such groups have gained wide acceptance throughout American history (The Advocacy Group 2000).

Perspectives on Techniques of Influence

Early pluralist theory in political science asserts that competition among groups is the sole process by which policy is formed, with Congress as the passive referee in his struggle. The legislative vote on any issue tends to represent the composition of strength, i.e. the balance of power among the contending groups at the moment of voting. Each interest group is assumed to be interested in only one policy: It offers a legislator campaign resources in exchange for or the expectation of future services. Moreover, a resource, here, is anything that can be used to sway the specific choices or the strategies of another individual. Thus, resources include money, in-kind services, volunteer labor, etc. (Denzau and Munger 1986).

While organized interests are not new in American politics, a number of trends have developed within the last three decades that have dramatically changed the way these groups emerge and the manner in which they seek to affect public policy (The Advocacy Group 2000). These ever-evolving groups have developed more effective techniques and tactics to influence policy-makers and gain benefits for their constituencies.

These tactics and techniques attack the various levels and branches of the government in an effort to articulate the concerns of their constituent members, with the hope and belief that their ideals and desires will somehow be approved or the ideals of opposing groups will be disapproved. Interest groups articulate political demands in the society and seek support for these demands into authoritative public policy by influencing the choices of political personnel, and the various processes of public-policy making and enforcement (Almond 1958:275).

This section of the chapter looks at the techniques used by these groups to gain measurable and positive results. The section is broken down into several subsections. Subsection one looks at general techniques used by interest groups. Subsection two looks at the influence and techniques utilized by interest groups to obtain benefits from the United States legislature—Congress. Subsection three looks at the intersection of presidential policy making and the executive branch and interest groups. Subsection four focuses on the influence that interest groups have on the formulation and interpretation of the law as it pertains to the Supreme Court and the American judiciary. Subsection five looks at the influence that money through PACs has had and continues to have on the political arena

General Techniques

According to Barker et al. (1999), the relative effectiveness of interest groups in the political process may be explained by a number of factors. Perhaps the most important factor is the nature of membership of the particular group (1999:182). Moreover, the resources and the specific actions used by these groups make for the effectiveness of an interest group in the manipulation of any political process or political decision. The political efficacy of a particular interest group seen through its chosen techniques and resources of influence are quite important when these groups approach decision-makers and make demands on the system.

These resources that groups can bring to bear in achieving their goals is another factor to consider in assessing their influence in the political process. These resources relate to such elements as leadership, money, size of group membership, and how the group is organized (structured) to carry on its business. Groups try to stimulate a favorable public opinion, for example, through the use of "propaganda" or "educational campaigns." Through electioneering, groups seek to influence election outcomes by supporting candidates who are favorable (or at least not opposed) to their goals. Group participation may take several forms. It may range from outright endorsement and support of particular candidates to outright opposition in other situations (Barker et al. 1999: 183). On the one hand, pressure groups use propaganda as a means of influencing public opinion. Propaganda is the manipulation of symbols for the influencing of public opinion to a particular point of view (Dillon 1942: 476). On the other hand, education is a systematic training of the mind through study and instruction (Dillon 1942:478). Education, then, differs from propaganda. It uses a different technique, and it is objective in purpose. Nevertheless, it may also be used by pressure groups as an instrument for informing the public about the facts of a given issue (Dillon 1942:478).

Lobbying is yet another form of influence that groups utilize. Groups may advocate particular positions through the use of individual lobbyists who seek to advance the goals of the organization by having face-to-face meetings with decision-makers or their surrogates (Dillon 1942:475). Pressure groups frequently make use of the lobby as an instrument for influencing legislatures or governmental agencies. According to Janda et al. (1995:344), pressure groups could participate in direct lobbying which relies on personal contact with policymakers. This interaction occurs when a lobbyist meets with a member of Congress, an agency official, or a staff member. Also, through indirect lobbying, Janda et al. state that these groups partake in grassroots lobbying which involves an interest group's rank-and-file members and may include people outside the organization who sympathize with its goals. Grassroots tactics, such as letter writing campaigns and protests, are often used in conjunction with direct lobbying (Janda et al. 1995:345). Moreover, these groups may participate in information campaigns, organized efforts to gain public backing by bringing group views to the public's attention (Janda et al. 1999: 346). Through the use of coalition building, several organizations band together for the purpose of lobbying. This joint effort conserves or makes more effective use of the resources of groups with similar views (1999:347).

One Against 435: Interest Groups and Congress

Interest groups tend to seek out the important points of access in the legislative process: the points where legislative policy is initiated and revised, voting and favorable action are possible (Almond 1958). The 435 members of the United States Congress are often times the foci of intense attention on the part of advocates for a particular issue. Each day, members of Congress are challenged by and influenced to make decisions amiable to a particular plural representation. Through varying activities, differing groups apply pressure on congresspersons to draft and pass perceived beneficial legislation or many times defeat perceived harmful legislation to a group's interests. This subsection looks at the techniques used by interest groups to manipulate the legislators to legislate in line with the interests of the group's constituency.

Through an analysis of the lobbying activities of the National Education Association during the spring and summer of 1977, Robert Smith (1984) advances one model of group influence. The development of a position by members on a legislative proposal depends significantly on two variables: their personal understanding of how the position affects the achievement of their goals and their public explanation of the position to interested audiences (Smith 1984:46). For the purposes of this chapter, following Smith, the aim of public explanations is to show how a position on a legislative proposal is consistent with the interests and preferences of interested audiences (Smith 1984:46). How a decision is made by the legislators will affect the society at-large and the group in particular. Furthermore, members, through the indirect and, at times, direct influence of interest groups, devise decisions that are in line with the group's desired outcome(s). Although congressional members are responsible for drafting legislation benefitting the entire nation, many policies are skewed in favor of a particular interest group.

These interest groups offer members varying scenarios to show the possible ramifications of their particular vote. These scenarios indirectly influence lawmakers to vote for the position advocated by the group. These groups provide arguments that establish various interpretations of the consequences of different positions on a legislative proposal. The aim is to show how the position favored by the advocate is also one that is consistent with the goals of the members—either by shaping the members' personal understandings of the consequences or by providing members with acceptable explanations of their presentations (Smith 1984: 47). Such presentations are also made in a variety of ways, including testimony before congressional committees, conversations with members or their staff assistants, and letter and telegram campaigns. Both interest group lobbyists and members of Congress, for example, see presentations as the most important activity for influencing the decisions of Congress (Smith 1984:48).

According to Mahood (2000), congresspersons are the focus of other means of influence just as effective. Among these is the generation or appearance of spontaneity: a ground swell of public opinion or widespread expressions of "public concern" over some time that have legitimacy but do not appear to be orchestrated (Mahood 2000:55).

Mahood also argues that through electioneering, these groups seek to influence lawmakers to make decisions favorable to group goals. These groups elect their friends and supporters to public office. Through mass "get out the vote" campaigns, groups are able to galvanize their members to elect members sympathetic to their causes when current members do not or have not acquiesced to their positions. This deepening commitment serves two purposes: (1) group support is a strong inducement for a candidate to support the association's goals, and (2) participation helps ensure that sympathetic officials remain in office (Mahood 2000: 55).

According to Rosenthal (1993:115), many relationships between lobbyists and legislators just happen notwithstanding the fact that some relationships are not left to chance. Interested parties focus on members who they view to be the most susceptible to group pressure and apply said pressure. Rosenthal believes that there exist ten methods most often used by interest groups to influence legislators. Though, on their face, these relationships are not *quid pro quo* per se, the resulting support of legislators leaves one to realize their effectiveness, nonetheless. The tactics are:

(1) Entertaining. Interest groups host special events where legislators are "wined and dined" in an effort to bring the policy makers and groups closer together.

(2) Trips. Groups often provide legislators with trips to various places and to different events.

(3) Gifts. Though often times the gifts are minimal, "it's the thought that counts."

(4) Athletics. Lobbyists and legislators partake in rounds of golf, a friendly game of basketball, or run a few miles together all in the name of building a better relationship.

(5) Constituent Services. Interest groups provide services to a legislator's constituency.

(6) Appreciation and acknowledgment. Many groups will host roasts and awards banquets in honor of chosen legislators to show their esteemed appreciation for their dubious service to the public.

(7) Understanding. Many groups will send lobbyists to become the legislators' "best friends," listening to their concerns and aiding them in non-professional ways.

(8) Advice. Many lobbyists will offer advice to legislators on varying issues not simply professional ones.

(9)　Assistance on legislation. Legislators will at times confer with lobbyists to make certain that some drafted legislation is in line with that group's particular goals.

(10)　Campaign contributions and involvement. Groups will provide manpower to ensure the election of a proponent (or defeat of an opponent) of the group's interests. Also, to be discussed more in-depth later, groups will provide direct financial assistance to a candidate to ensure his/her victory (Rosenthal 1993: 115-120).

Interest Groups and the Oval Office:
Influencing the Executive

Although most attention is focused on the legislature, as the executive branch of government expands and its role in policymaking further develops, groups have begun to utilize techniques to influence the presidency, the offices of the president, and the bureaucracy. According to Mahood (2000:63), given the dramatic size and growth of the executive branch over the past quarter century, it is not surprising that it is an increasing target for group penetration.

As the modern presidency draws more policy issues directly into the White House domain, the opportunity for groups to secure explicit communications with the president or presidential surrogates becomes an increasingly precious commodity (Peterson 1992). Offering support, not to mention money and votes, interest groups and presidents enjoy a relationship of mutual benefit. According to Peterson, there exist two foci between the executive and interest groups: a programmatic focus and a representational focus. The first focuses on the programmatic element of the administration that would benefit the group and in turn the presidency. The other emphasizes an administration's desire to reinforce its political standing (Peterson 1992:613). Through either direct or indirect lobbying, groups apply the needed force on the executive to elicit a positive political response. Also, groups lobby bureaucratic units to apply pressure on the president to either take or not take a particular action. This pressure could include the threat of electoral backlash, which may affect the reelectability of a president (Mahood 2000:107).

Interest Groups and the Bench:
Influencing the Judiciary

Although the Constitution supposedly established a system that does not allow the influence of outside entities into the halls of the judiciary, there are ways that interest groups advance their positions and seek to gain favorable results from the courts. Other than the lobbying of Congress, litigation, a direct approach to influencing the federal judiciary (Mahood 2000:120), has been the other most productive and lucrative tactic used by groups.

Among the most effective means of influencing the judiciary has been the use of *Amicus Curiae* briefs or friend of the court briefs that represent a more indirect route to judicial influence. Amicus briefs are interest group inputs to court personnel of additional data and arguments relevant to an impending judicial decision (Mahood 2000: 123). Participation as amicus curiae has long been an important tactic of organized interests in litigation before the United States Supreme Court (Caldeira and Wright 1988:1109). Each year, multitudes of interest groups participate in various guises before the Supreme Court. It is clear that in the last couple of decades interest groups have stepped up their activities before the courts, just as they have in other political arenas. Interest groups can of course choose to take part before the Supreme Court in many different roles, and they most often do so as amici curiae (Caldeira and Wright 1988:1109-1110). The tactics groups can use to influence legislation are considerable, including participating in "class actions" and test cases, participating as amici curiae, giving advice and service, providing expert testimony and financial assistance, and taking control of the law suit (Caldeira and Wright 1988:1110).

The use of the courts has been a well-documented technique of groups. Vose (1959) blazed a trail with his meticulous and intriguing case study of how the National Association for the Advancement of Colored People (NAACP) Legal Defense Fund used a variety of strategies and tactics in its campaign of litigation to end the restrictive covenant in housing (Caldeira and Wright 1988: 1110).

Moreover, members of the Court use the participation of organized interests as amici curiae prior to certiorari or jurisdiction as an indicator of the importance of a case among those other than the immediate parties (McGuire and Caldeira 1993:718). Scholars have demonstrated over and over again the vigorous, extensive, and continuing efforts on the part of interest groups to lobby the courts. So, clearly, interest groups have used the vehicle of amicus briefs often and, in recent years, with increased frequency. There is, in addition, some fragmentary evidence that participation as amicus curiae constitutes an efficacious route for interest groups to take in their attempt to influence the Court (Caldreira and Wright 1988: 1110-1111).

Money and Influence:
PACs and Soft Money

Political Action Committees (PACs) are organizations that collect contributions from particular classes of individuals for the purpose of influencing elections. The rationale is that, by aggregating small donations from a large number of contributors, similarly situated people can maximize the effect of their money (Rosenthal 1993:133).

According to Rosenthal (1993:134-136), PACs have grown in numbers, resources, and market share since the 1970s. PACS have several motives for their development, which include:

(a) to show support for and to help elect friends;
(b) to oppose and to help defeat those who are not friends;
(c) to support those who are likely to be reelected, especially those who exercise considerable influence;

(d) to gain or improve access to members, particularly influential
ones; and

(e) to attempt to change the odds by affecting the overall outcome
of an election.

PAC officials use one of two basic strategies when attempting to influence congressional outcomes through campaign contributions. Under one strategy, PACs attempt to influence elections. This strategy gives priority to candidates in the closest contests, and the objective is to keep representatives in office, or to place new candidates in office, who by nature are most sympathetic to the PAC's policy goals. Under the other strategy, PACs attempt to influence the behavior of incumbent representatives (Wright 1985:402-403).

An increasingly important dimension of player involvement in campaign finance is "soft money" (contributions by national parties to state parties to encourage greater voter participation through registration, party building, and get-out-the-vote drives) (Mahood 2000: 82). These contributions are usually made without an explicit *quid pro quo* (Mahood 2000:83). Organizations also use soft money allocations to distribute information and have commercials and other forms of support outlets to advance the candidacy of a particular person or seek public approval of a particular issue.

DC Vote: Getting Its Message Across

According to Amy W. Slemmer, Executive Director of DC Vote, the organization has accepted the mantle of leadership in the fight for Washington, DC residents to obtain full representation in the United States Congress. While in attendance at the DC Delegate breakfast at the Democratic National Convention during the summer of 2000, Slemmer solicited the support of the attendees in DC Vote's efforts to challenge the centuries-old disenfranchisement of District residents. This section outlines the various techniques used by DC Vote to gain support, change opinion, and galvanize its following to obtain congressional representation.

Education

As previously discussed, interest groups rely on various techniques to influence decision-makers. One of the most effective and most used techniques is education. According to Dillon (1942), education is the systematic training of the minds of those important people an interest group believes can have an effect on the goals of the organization. First and foremost, DC Vote is dedicated to educating DC residents and other American citizens on the unfair reality that the second highest per capita taxed region, one of the most populated areas that would constitute one of the largest of the smaller states in terms of population, and one of the richest enclaves of United States citizens in the country are not represented by any voting member in the United States Congress. Through letter writing campaigns, DC Vote has been effective in getting out its message. DC Vote sends letters to DC residents and strategic people in other areas who can possibly influence decision-makers.

The DC Vote Speakers Bureau is a critical component of the organization's effort to inform the public about the groundswell of support for its issue and to let people know how they can get involved. The bureau provides speakers for student groups, house party fundraisers, gatherings of civic, religious, and community organizations, and any other individuals or organizations that would like to learn more about its effort to finally put an end to the 200 years of disenfranchisement that the citizens of Washington, DC have suffered (www.dcvote.org). Speakers are influential scholars, political advocates, and/or legal minds with beneficial opinions or inputs for the DC Vote mission. The Bureau goes to various places in Washington, DC and across the country seeking to validate the claims that DC residents are entitled to representation in Congress.

DC Vote sponsors door-to-door literature distribution and neighborhood canvassing efforts. Led by Dennis Jackson, these activities get information to local residents so that when challenges are made to DC Vote, they will have an educated and united, not to mention large, vocal following.

These grassroots tactics, such as the letter writing campaigns and canvassing protests, are effective in gaining support and more importantly, attention from the national media and other persons outside of the District who can apply pressure to decision-makers.

Fundraising

DC Vote hosts House Parties, where hosts bring together interested groups and concerned individuals to discuss issues of importance to the organization. Also, these House Parties provide DC Vote with the opportunity to raise money and gain increased volunteer support.

Piggy-back fundraising, according to Joseph Sternlieb, President of DC Vote, "is a unique effort." DC Vote places more than 2,000 DC Vote return envelopes into campaign contribution solicitation requests of local activists, lobbyists and donors. The return envelopes ask those people solicited to donate money to the organization and use the envelope to resubmit payment to the organization. Since DC residents give more money per capita to United States Senate and House candidates, it is quite effective soliciting through these mailings. Those reached vary from across the political spectrum and ideologies.

DC Vote has adopted "Taxation without Representation" as its official slogan. Most important, this slogan has been embroidered on t-shirts, hats, embossed on bumper stickers, buttons, and key chains. Lastly, through an effective lobbying campaign, DC Vote has convinced Mayor Anthony Williams to change District license plates to read "taxation without representation." The new plates are meant to show the world the peculiar situation in which DC residents find themselves. Moreover, DC Vote has distributed a video to further educate people on the mission of the organization and how it would be best utilized in the organization's quest.

The organization seeks and obtains endorsements from political leaders, current elected officials, and prominent citizens to their cause.

These endorsements add needed leverage to the claims that DC Vote makes on those in decision-making positions. Congresspersons, university presidents, legal and academic scholars are sought after to provide support and guidance (see Chapter 4 for more on DC Vote's fundraising techniques).

Direct Lobbying

As Janda et al. mention, lobbying is an effective means for applying pressure on decision-makers (1995:345). DC Vote has participated in direct and indirect lobbying techniques. Members of the organization have met with congresspersons and policy-makers from both major political parties in an effort to influence them to support congressional action to grant DC residents congressional representation. Their most noticeable proponent has been Delegate Eleanor Holmes-Norton of the District of Columbia. During her address before the 2000 Democratic National Convention, District residents chanted "taxation without representation," while holding signs bearing the same slogan. More importantly, Norton, during her address, denounced the disenfranchisement of District residents and called on the federal government to allow the hundreds of thousands of residents to participate fully in the democratic process (see Chapter 6 for additional information on DC Vote's targets of influence).

Amicus Curiae

DC Vote, in the recent *Alexander v Mineta* (2000) case before the United States Supreme Court, filed a "friend of the court" brief in support of Washington, DC representation. Although the Court ruled against the organization and the District, DC Vote provided needed history and input to the proponent arguments before the High Court.

Electioneering

DC Vote has vowed to support any and all candidates who support its ideals and mission. For instance, Democratic-presidential nominee Albert Gore, Jr. endorsed voting rights for the District and, consequently, the organization leant its support to the local election campaign of Al Gore.

Conclusion

In general, the relative effectiveness of interest groups in the political process may be explained by a number of factors (Barker et al. 1999: 182). The previous chapter has outlined the legitimacy, frequency, and efficacy of the major forms of activity undertaken by interest groups to gain benefits from perceived decision-makers for their members from the three branches of the federal government. The *resources* that groups can bring to bear in achieving their goals are another factor to consider in assessing their influence in the political process. These resources relate to such elements as leadership, money, size of group membership, and how the group is organized (structured) to carry on its business. Of course, in this respect, strategy and tactics, that is, how and in what manner groups actually use their resources, are directly and crucially related to group effectiveness (Barker et al. 1999:183).

As the previous chapter showed, DC Vote has performed as many other groups in its activities to persuade decision-makers to grant the franchise to the citizens of Washington, DC. Unfortunately, DC Vote has had successes in some areas, while measurable failures in others.

DC Vote has been tremendously successful in educating the general public and the public at-large about the history of DC disenfranchisement and the reasons this is not only unfair, but also possibly unconstitutional. The education campaign undertaken by DC Vote has been quite successful because it has been national in scope. DC Vote has been successful in the unification of like-minded individuals behind a common purpose—the granting of full congressional representation to Washington, DC residents.

Moreover, DC Vote has lobbied the executive branch, calling on both major political parties to grant citizens of the Nation's Capital the ability to chose their leaders within the United States Congress. DC Vote has joined, in the form of amicus curiae, the ranks of community activists and other concerned citizens in their effort to bring suit before the Supreme Court. Although ultimately overruled by the High Court, DC Vote, while lobbying the legislative and executive branches, has been, albeit unsuccessful, instrumental in judicial challenges.

By employing the various techniques of influence from lobbying to education to electioneering and campaign contributions to litigation, DC Vote, like so many other interest groups, arguably has been somewhat successful in making demands on the system with the intent of accruing benefits for its members. Since the group is recent, its efficacy is measurably limited; however, its motivation and following are growing. The efficacy of the group's techniques increases more and more, as the group applies ample pressure on those who can grant reprise to the disenfranchisement of Washington, DC residents.

There is considerable disagreement among learned individuals about the most efficacious means to achieve organizational goals; however, most scholars agree that a combined approach of the most puissant tactics is highly recommended. DC Vote, like other interest groups, has been successful in weaving together a distinct tapestry of strategies aimed at the specific foci in the political arena with the requisite authority to lift the yolk of representational impotence from around the necks of Washington, DC residents.

CHAPTER 6

▼

TARGETS OF INFLUENCE

Kathy Booh

Introduction

In 1978, both the both the United States House of Representatives and the United States Senate approved the DC Voting Rights constitutional amendment by two-thirds majority of their legislatures. If approved by three-fourths of the states within seven years, the amendment would have granted the residents of the District of Columbia full representation in Congress. By the deadline in 1985, however, the amendment failed when only sixteen of the required thirty-eight states ratified it.

Eight years later, in 1993, the United States House of Representatives defeated a bill that would have made the District of Columbia the 51st state of the Union. In spite of the 277-153 votes decision, supporters of DC's quest for congressional representation (such as DC Delegate Eleanor

Holmes Norton and Reverend Jesse Jackson) were glad that it raised awareness about the issue. For years, they had defended the right of 600,000 federal tax-paying citizens to receive equal representation in Congress. Former DC Delegate Walter Fauntroy had called DC "the nation's last colony." On the other side of the issue, opponents have always used the United States Constitution to point out the capital's special status. Partisanship may also play a role among the policymakers: since DC primarily votes Democratic, Republicans have traditionally been opposed to granting DC representation in order to prevent Democrats from gaining additional voting seats in the two chambers.

This chapter looks at the targets DC Vote seeks to influence the most in its crusade. Mahood defines "targeting" as "communicating specifically drafted messages to a specific segment of the population" (2000:157). In this particular case, it is important for the leaders of DC Vote to determine the forces that have the power to make or break legislation. Who are the major power players/decision makers? What responses from these policymakers and institutions affect the cause of DC Vote? These questions are thoroughly probed in the rest of the chapter.

Existing Perspectives on Targets of Influence

As any lobby group, DC Vote understands that it is essential to identify the different key players who are most important to the issues it cares about. It is vital for interest groups to target policymakers who are members of the legislative branch, and, to a lesser but still important degree, government officials who are part of the executive agencies.

The power players who can make the most difference in helping the cause of a lobby group like DC Vote are primarily congressional leaders, committee members and congressional staff personnel. The presiding officers in Congress have the ability to influence members on the particular issues lobbyists are determined to see addressed. As far as interest groups are concerned, Capitol Hill is the place where things happen in terms of legislation. Mahood points out how much Congress has evolved since the 1940s, as follows:

> In the old Congress, a small but powerful elite monopolized the party leadership and committee chairs and generally ran the business of each chamber.... Life "on the Hill" was relatively slower, more personal, and more collegial...[In the late sixties], the new members were self-starters and policy-oriented. They came to Capitol Hill to legislate.... Advocates of social issues have relatively greater potential for access and policy influence (Mahood 2000:94-95).

Another factor that affects congressional leadership is the level of bipartisanship that is more present in the Senate than in the House of Representatives:

> Votes are rarely along strict party lines, except on the most highly charged and politicized issues, such as the budget, major presidential nominees, significant foreign policy issues, or campaign finance reform.... A lobbyist therefore has greater leverage on an issue in the Senate than can be expected in the House" (Wolpe and Levine 1996:25-26)

Committees are the most important venue in which legislators operate. They mark the first step in the enactment of laws. Experts do emphasize that if one loses in a committee, it is more difficult to win on the floor. But once a bill is passed to the floor, it is rarely defeated. "A victory in committee creates a precedent and momentum that place a heavier burden on those seeking to reverse it at the next stage of the process.... What happens in committee is almost the single most important determinant of success or failure" (Wolpe and Levine 1996:23). As pointed out earlier, partisanship affects the way laws are administered. House committees are traditionally more partisan than House panels. There is no doubt that when the House is firmly under the control of one party, it is harder for a minority member to prevail in committee without some strong support from the majority party. On the other hand, Senate committees tend to display less intensity and antagonisms along party lines.

Lobbyists spend a substantial amount of time dealing with congressional staff members in their attempt to gain influence over the legislators. Congress currently employs over 20,000 staff members, researchers and others, expecting from them more than just clerical work.

> It is not uncommon for staff personnel to attend and advise members during committee or subcommittee hearings and later markups. Many have expertise in various policy areas.... They are literally the 'eyes,', 'ears,' and even the 'brain' of current members.... Staff personnel draft legislation, conduct policy research, and indulge in a lot of parliamentary negotiation on behalf of their members as well as coalition building (Mahood 2000:97).

Lobbyists do value to a great extent the importance of gaining access to staff members in order to influence members of the legislatures. "Winning the confidence of the staff—and maintaining it thereafter—is a prerequisite to an ongoing, successful political relationship with any political office" (Wolpe and Levine 1996:16).

For lobbyists, there was a time when Capitol Hill was the only place worth a trip to get things done in terms of pushing for legislation. There was a certain disdain for bureaucracy among lobbies. But today, the executive branch of government has become a growing target of interest groups' agenda. "National bureaucrats, once in office, serve as liaisons both to Congress and the interest group community...They serve as gatekeepers to national policymaking" (Mahood 2000:65). Unlike in Congress, where ideology and party affiliation rule, partisanship along the president's party is key in the bureaucracy. Executive officials work for the president's agenda first and foremost. The system of checks and balances allows the president and his administration to be key players in enacting laws, thus being useful agents in the objectives of lobbies. The executive branch can be a major force in determining legislative outcomes. As far as lobbyists are concerned, there are tremendous opportunities to form alliances with the executive policymaking system in their pursuit of influence over congressional committee members. Compared to targeting congressional officials, lobbying bureaucrats is still a relatively new phenomenon. The Office of Public Liaisons (OPL)—which was established in 1974—facilitates access to the White House and the Commander-in-Chief. Interaction between lobbies and the OPL staff members may lead to a meeting with the president in person to address particular concerns surrounding an issue. Such an encounter can potentially attract the kind of media coverage that helps to raise national awareness regarding an issue such as AIDS, landmine or the education system.

To be most effective in its quest for full voting representation for the residents of the District of Columbia, DC Vote understands the necessity to reach out to those forces in the public sector that have the ability to pass legislation in its favor. So, the ultimate question becomes the following: How does DC Vote target those it believes are influential to meet its goal?

DC Vote's Targets of Influence

An analysis of interviews conducted with DC Vote officials and the organization's writings reveal many groups that DC Vote targets to promote its cause. The following is a summary of the findings on each group.

United States Congress

In 1996, Reverend Jesse Jackson, who was then the unofficial statehood Senator for the District of Columbia, stated the "the votes for statehood are not in the District, but in the Congress" (*Jet Magazine* July 22, 1996:6). When asked, DC Vote Executive Director Amy Slemmer who the most important targets of her organization were, she too primarily cited the two congressional houses, saying that congressional representatives need to be more aware of DC's lack of voting representation. Slemmer, who has been a DC resident for 15 years, deplores the fact that one of the first acts of the Republican Congress after its 1994 electoral victory was to show its hostility toward the District by stripping away Eleanor Holmes-Norton's voice in Congress. But the Republican takeover of Congress has not ended all hopes to see DC residents being granted full voting rights: "This not an issue for one particular party. It is a human rights issue that crosses over all political and ideological boundaries" (DC Vote Newsletter, September 2000).

To the delight of Slemmer and her organization, Norton said that she plans to introduce two new bills in the next session of Congress: one would provide DC residents with congressional voting rights; the second would suspend federal taxation on DC residents until voting rights are granted. Another supporter of DC Vote's cause, Mayor Anthony Williams, called for a citywide Mobilization Meeting on November 28, 2000, in which citizens were encouraged to exchange their opinions on the issue. And even though DC Vote representatives have not yet brought their case to Capitol Hill, they keep working closely with delegate Norton as well as with members of the DC subcommittee who deal with the DC Appropriations Bill.

The Executive Branch

DC Vote does not particularly target the executive branch of government. Its main goal is still primarily to reach the members of congress to push for legislation. As stated earlier, lobbying the executive is still a new, yet growing, phenomenon in American politics. Slemmer, though, insists that targeting Congress is what can bring full voting rights for DC Citizens to fruition. During his eight-year tenure, President Clinton showed that the DC cause was not one his administration's top priorities. In his 1992 campaign, he had stated that "to protect rights for all," he would "support statehood for the District of Columbia." But in 1993, it was reported that he had backed off his promise, which angered and disappointed many of his DC supporters.

During the 2000 presidential campaign, Senator and former candidate Bill Bradley made a statement in which he fully endorsed voting representation in Congress for DC residents. DC Vote President Joseph Sternlieb applauded Bradley for being the first major party candidate to highlight the issue in that election, and he urged the other presidential candidates to lend their support as well. It may not be surprising that Democratic candidate Al Gore favored DC voting rights while Republican candidate George W. Bush was against it.

The Judiciary

The *Alexander v Daley* Supreme Court case was a litigation in which DC Vote was involved. For eleven months, a three-judge panel considered the plaintiffs' case to grant full congressional representation to the residents of the District of Columbia. Another case, *Adams v Clinton,* in which DC Vote did not take part, dealt with making it possible for DC residents to either choose statehood or to unite with another state in representation matters. On March 20, 2000, the federal court panel ruled 2-1 against the plaintiffs, therefore against the right to voting representation.

Amy Slemmer commented that to win its case, DC Vote has to target primarily the legislative process rather than the courts. Therefore, the judiciary branch of government is not a major target of influence by the organization.

The Press

Slemmer identifies the media as being one of DC Vote's targets. Local and national exposure can only bring more awareness regarding the issue. Media outlets such as the *Washington Post*, the *Washington Times,* and the *New York Times* often run stories relating to DC's plight. On February 8, 2000, the *Washington Post*, in a lead editorial, contended its long-held opinion that "District residents have a right to be represented in the legislature that governs them." This type of endorsement to the DC cause is beneficial in raising awareness among the public and political leaders, as well as in putting more pressure on Congress, which is DC Vote's chief target.

Residents Outside the District

As a political as well as educational organization, DC Vote also focuses on spreading the word outside the District's boundaries and providing information to the people who live in the 50 states, so that they can put pressure on their congressional representatives on behalf of the District of Columbia. One step to raise such awareness is the distribution of DC license plates that read "NO TAXATION WITHOUT REPRESENTATION." Slemmer is hopeful that the message would reach as many American residents outside DC as possible.

Civil Rights Activists

Some of the supporters of the cause of DC Vote are political activists who are also board members of the organization, such as Carolyn Jefferson-Jenkins (President of the League of Women Voters of the United-States), Elizabeth Martin (President of the League of Women Voters of the District of Columbia), Scott Harshbarger (President of Common Cause), Wade Henderson (Executive Director of the Leadership Conference on Civil Rights), and Kathy Schmidt (co-chair of the DC Advisory Committee). Other organizations that work closely with DC Vote are the National Association for the Advancement of Colored People (NAACP), as well as the National Council of Negro Women.

Church Organizations

One body of influence that appears to be a major force in lobbying is the church leadership. In the case of DC Vote, Amy Slemmer cites Attorney and seminary student Mark Schaefer as an exemplary figure (DC Vote Newsletter, April 2000). Schaefer, who has been an active DC Vote

board member since 1998, has contributed to secure support for DC Vote
from national church organizations. He organized the Foundry
Democratic Project, which passed a resolution calling on the United
Methodist Church, the White House and Congress to declare its support
for full democratic rights to DC residents. In May 2000, the General
Conference of the United Methodist Church voted in favor of the resolution to support full voting rights, adding that "the disenfranchisement of
the citizens of the District of Columbia is an egregious moral wrong,
which must be rectified." Therefore, having the full endorsement of a
powerful church organization can only help DC Vote's goal to educate
people, bring awareness, and push for legislation that would ensure voting
rights for DC residents.

Conclusion

In the general literature on interest groups, the legislative and executive
branches of government are identified as being the primary targets of lobbyists. In the case of DC Vote, however, congressional representatives are
the most important group of people to deal with in order to gain support
and to redress the situation. Reaching the legislative process, rather than
the bureaucracy and the court system, is the key component of DC Vote's
agenda.

The outcome of the contested 2000 presidential election will not deter
DC Vote's resilience as to their hopes of one day achieving a goal it deeply
believes to be righteous. As stated earlier, a substantial amount of support
outside the government keeps raising awareness surrounding the plight of
DC residents and, thus, puts pressure on legislators to respond effectively
to the particular matter.

EPILOGUE

---▼---

PROSPECTS FOR VOTING RIGHTS

Ray M. Crawford, Jr.

Introduction

The future voting rights within the United States Nation's Capital, Washington DC, is no closer to being defined than it was ten, twenty, or even two hundred years ago. In 1800, citizens of the District of Columbia still had the privilege to vote for representatives to state and national offices and to be active participants in the state governments of Maryland or Virginia, respectively, as well as the United States Government. Today, the District of Columbia barely governs itself, having to forward all laws passed by its governing body, comprised of a City Council and Mayor, to Congress for review. Within Congress, the District of Columbia holds one seat in the House of Representatives for a non-voting delegate and no seats, voting or non-voting, in the Senate. Is the future to remain status quo, or will the citizens of Washington DC be granted voting rights? The prospects for voting rights may not illustrate immediate acquisition; how-ever, initiatives for change have been presented and must be summarily addressed by the President and Congress within the next few years.

When examining the *prospects* of voting rights in DC, the term *prospects* must be clearly defined. The *prospects* with regard to this chapter are, thus, defined as any initiative, be it special interest group or derivative thereof, having the potential for successfully acquiring equal voting representation in Congress for the citizens of the District of Columbia. However, to state that there are various prospects, or rather special interest groups with the capacity for potential success, promotes the assumption that collectively these groups could establish a stronger position for voting rights and be successful in attaining them. This assumption may bear some truth if these interest groups were synonymous in typology, having similar moti-vational, purposive and economic benefits. Although voting rights may be a common thread, the typology of these interest groups is varying, as are the benefits associated with their respective initiatives.

The greatest difference between the ideologies of interest groups regarding the acquisition of voting rights is the method by which these rights will be attained. The two preeminent ideals are statehood and congressional repre-sentation. But are these two ideals the same? Though both ideals share in the goal of attaining voting rights, they are not the same. Statehood will provide Washingtonians with fair representation in Congress, but it would also reshape the District's governmental framework entirely. Congressional repre-sentation alone could be achieved through an amendment to the Constitution, but it would still subject Washington to the less than demo-cratic governing body presently in place. Statehood deals with full democracy for Washington, inclusive of the same rights and privileges enjoyed by all states in the Union: the whole pie. An amendment granting congressional representation would be a limited form of democracy for Washington at best, a mere slice of the whole pie. There is even the belief that singly gaining rep-resentation may thwart any efforts at achieving statehood. These ideals are examined further throughout this chapter.

Within the discussion of statehood versus congressional representation lie a distinct illustration of the differences between the two and, perhaps, the prospect with the greatest potential for immediate success. This prospect is called a lawsuit, or in this case lawsuits. The first is *Adams v Clinton*, more commonly titled as Twenty DC Citizens versus Clinton. The second is *Alexander v Daley*. Both of these suits were filed by citizens of Washington, DC against the United States government, and both entailed the request for voting rights. Yet, like the ideals discussed earlier, the method by which these rights are to be attained is different. In short, the case of *Adams v Clinton* was a suit brought by twenty citizens for equal protection of their rights as designated to citizens by the United States Constitution directly against the office of the president. The theory of *equal protection* is inclusive of the majority of provisions that statehood ideal would provide to citizens of Washington, DC. To win a decision in this case would provide a firm foundation for the passage of a statehood amendment in Congress. The *Alexander v Daley* case was a suit filed by citizens against the United States Congress for representation equal to voting seats within. This case demands representation in singular form, and does not request changes in governmental framework, i.e. the congressional representation ideal. Will the outcome of these lawsuits set a precedent for future voting rights in Washington DC? To be victorious in both or either would definitely have an impact, as stated earlier, but to lose these decisions will not dissolve the issue of voting rights.

The voting rights issue may never dissolve, because it has been unresolved since the beginning of the 19th century. Citizens liken their plight to the Revolutionary war and a slogan most appropriately adopted by many interest groups has been *Taxation without Representation*. Journalists have labeled Washington, DC the *Last Colony* in reference to the federal rule over the city and its local government. In comparison with such criticism, there have been differing opinions on this issue within the federal government; even President Clinton stated that the citizens of Washington, DC should be allowed some type of voting rights. Yet initiatives and amendments have failed. As recently as 1985, a voting rights amendment met its demise, suffering from a congressional defeat that equated to less than half of the required states supporting. The prospects of Washington, DC voting rights are examined within this chapter by identifying the various interest groups that have taken on the issue, directly or indirectly, discussing the probable outcome of the two lawsuits seeking these same rights, highlighting the various solutions to include statehood and congressional representation, and finally weighing the varying perspectives on the immediate future. There are numerous prospects, but what bearing these will have on the immediate acquisition of voting rights lies in the pages ahead.

Existing Perspectives on the Prospects for DC Voting Rights

The most pertinent issue regarding voting rights for Washington, DC is by what means these rights will be attained. There are numerous ways to conceivably incorporate Washington, DC into Congress, but there are three approaches that have been discussed as feasible. These are: retrocession, a full voting rights amendment, and statehood. The Web site for DC Vote, the Coalition for DC Representation in Congress, have these ideologies listed as the solutions to the problem. But which one of these varying schools of thought is most likely to succeed? First, each must be discussed.

Washington, DC was carved out of two states, Maryland and Virginia, in 1787. Although the District was to be established as an independent body, for some time, the citizens within continued to exercise voting rights within their former states. The section of land that came from Virginia, now known as Arlington, was returned in 1846. The process by which this land was returned to Virginia is called retrocession. The section of land that came form Maryland was never returned, and this is what currently makes up Washington, DC. However, if the legislature in Maryland were to allow the nonfederal section of Washington, DC to be returned to the state, then voting rights would also be returned to the citizens, as residents of Maryland (dcvote.org/solution.htm). Washington, DC would also have state and federal support and protection. The District has many functions that mirror the responsibilities of independent states; but with retrocession, it would be relieved of those functions and integrated into the framework of the Maryland State government. The economic limitations placed on the District by the federal government would also dissolve, allowing for more economic growth for the city. Still, initiatives for retrocession have been little more than just that, initiatives and not actions. The lack of action stems from the surplus of opposition.

Those who support statehood for Washington, DC are strongly opposed to retrocession. It would be a total defeat in the struggle for statehood and would decrease the District residents' power in the political arena. Not only do statehood advocates oppose retrocession, but also so do residents and government officials in Maryland. According to a survey in 1990, 82% of the state delegates in Maryland and 92% of the state senators responding were in opposition of retrocession (narpac.org/ITXGU06A.HTM). Residents of the District are as strongly against retrocession as residents of Maryland. It would compromise the identity of the city by placing a predominantly African-American enclave into a state that will not recognize the needs of those African-American citizens in the same way, because they will be the minority.

In 1978, a Full Voting Rights Amendment was proposed. The amendment was not for allowing Washington, DC the rights of a state, but for allowing the citizens full voting rights for congressional representation. Yet, even though the amendment passed Congress and was supported by President Jimmy Carter, it was only ratified by 16 states while needing 38 states to ratify for passage. Those in support of an amendment for voting rights want enfranchisement for citizens now, and they feel that an amendment is an expeditious means to this end. However, those opposed have a different opinion regarding the right to enfranchisement for Washingtonians. Their argument is that the forefathers never had intentions of providing voting rights to District citizens, and that there are larger cities and counties throughout this nation that do not have independent representation. Others feel that an amendment will no resolve the problems stemming from a lack of structural government in the District, and that it will also negate efforts for more inclusive means of achieving representation.

The United States Constitution empowers Congress to admit Washington, DC into the Union as a state. Article IV, Section 3 of the Constitution says, "New states may be admitted by Congress into this Union." The Constitution does not put parameters on that statement, which allows Congress the power to determine criteria for admission to the Union. In short, Congress can make statehood possible with some simple legislation. If the District were made the 51st state, it would be entitled to two seats in the Senate and at least one in the House of Representatives. Paul Whipple summarizes the ideals of the numerous proponents for statehood best:

> Only under statehood would the people of the District achieve full citizenship. Freedom to tax and to spend without Congressional restriction and control over its executive, legislative and judicial powers would come from statehood. A new state is on equal footing with all others in the Union. A state may not leave the Union, nor may its status of equality be altered. Neither may a state be abolished without the consent of the states and the Congress. Constitutional amendments, on the other hand, can be repealed. Home rule, granted by Congress, can be altered or withdrawn. Only statehood is permanent (1984:6).

The arguments against statehood are strong and varying. Many who oppose statehood say that the District is a city, not having the size and population to warrant statehood. They also argue that Washington, DC is not an independent entity but actually a possession of the United States and is, thus, common property of all citizens within the country. An even larger obstacle is the fact that, currently, the economy in the District is very dependent upon federal funds for operation, making it difficult to see from where the revenue would come to support all the functions of a state.

There is finally the proposition that Washington, DC is not ready for statehood. There has been so much corruption and poor management blemishing the past record of Washington, DC that is necessary for a period of time to pass without such negative occurrences for the issue of statehood to truly be taken seriously (Best 1984:216-219).

Still, despite its detractors, the statehood debate may hold the most favorable outcome regarding voting rights. Statehood promotes discussion throughout the realm of American politics. Even President Clinton acknowledged his support of voting rights for the citizens of Washington, DC. On March 28, 2000, President Clinton provided a statement to Delegate Eleanor Holmes Norton verifying this fact. An excerpt form his statement follows:

> I have long made clear my support for statehood for the District of Columbia. One of the most important attributes of statehood is the right to elect Senators and Representatives. My administration will continue to work with all members of the District community to find the best means of achieving that goal...for American democracy (house.gov/Norton/pr00329.htm).

If the President supported voting rights, then why is Washington, DC still without them? The President is but a piece of the federal governmental framework, and his lone support cannot change the current state of District representation. However, his statement illustrates the entire issue eloquently. The core issue is representation for the citizens of Washington, DC in Congress. The President and his administration, Democrats, support statehood for the District, which, as previously stated, poses the strongest argument for representation to be achieved in Congress. Yet voting rights are not a reality, which identifies that there is a division surrounding the issue of voting rights that surpasses mere public opinion and legislative reformation. Where does the division begin? The perspectives of political parties may lend some valuable information.

Historically, the Democratic Party has supported the right of suffrage for the District of Columbia. The first time voting rights for Washington, DC became a part of the Democratic Party's political platform was during the 1940s under President Harry Truman. Truman believed in self-government for Washington, DC, and he felt that the lack thereof was an injustice to the citizens who resided in the city. However, although legislation was proposed to establish "home-rule" in the District, and supported by the President and the Senate, it met strong opposition in the House of Representatives, which was predominantly Republican (narpac.org/ITGU06A.HTM). Yet at the onset of the Civil Rights Movement, the District did make progress in regard to voting rights. In 1960, the Twenty-Third Amendment was proposed which would allow the District three electoral votes towards the election of the United States President. The amendment was ratified in 1961. The progress was limited because Washington, DC remained without any representation in Congress.

Part of the reason progress remained minimal is due to the fact that the bipartisan division remains constant. Statehood, which encompasses total representation for the District, has continued to be endorsed by the Democratic Party within presidential platforms dating back to the 1984 campaign. In contrast, the Republican Party does not merely oppose statehood, but it argues that it is not an ideal that corresponds to the original intent of the Constitution and suggests that statehood is illegal for Washington, DC. Such a firm position against statehood is logically opposition to equal representation for Washingtonians. But there is more to this opposition than the simple interpretation of Constitutional intent.

> The electorate in the District of Columbia is 78 percent Democratic, followed by independents who compromise 12 percent. The percentage of Republican voters is only 8 percent…Under these circumstances, its representatives to

Congress are almost certain to be Democratic...the Republican members of Congress would have little incentive to vote for statehood under these conditions (Harris 1995:223).

It is logical to assume that Democrats support statehood for Washingtonians because the representation will increase the number of Democratic votes in Congress; the Republicans oppose representation for the same reason. Comparatively, no matter what approach is discussed with regard to representation, the division will remain constant. This division not only lies upon political party lines, but racial lines as well. In the words of Whipple,

The largest black city in America is being told it can't have the same rights as other cities and its mostly black officials are being told that their power is properly limited. It's the biggest affirmative action case in America, but no one takes it to court because it's constitutional (Whipple 1984:8).

Washington, DC has over 500,000 residents and approximately 70% are African-American. The ratio of registered Democrats to Republicans is nearly 10 to 1. It is highly probable that if Washington, DC acquired congressional representation, those representatives would be African-American Democrats, increasing the power of both the African-American voice and Democratic vote in Congress. Is this issue of race the sole reason that voting rights have not been granted to Washington, DC? No, but it is a factor that must be identified when discussing voting rights in the District. No matter how many ideologies exist regarding equal representation/voting rights for the citizens of the Nation's Capital, none can dismiss the direct effects representation will have on the racial dynamics of the federal governing body, the underlying color of perspective.

Findings on DC Vote

One citizen's perspective on voting rights cannot change the situation for all citizens within the District of Columbia, be it legitimate or otherwise. But if that one citizen can take that perspective and influence others, to the extent where one citizen multiplies into a group of citizens with a common perspective, that perspective or interest increases in legitimacy, as does the influence of the entire group. American politics, defined as an ongoing struggle for influence (Mahood 2000: 1), is a menagerie of interest groups. Human rights organizations, labor unions and political parties are all forms of interest groups, each founded in an effort to articulate the concerns of their respective members.

In an effort to articulate the need for the citizens of the District of Columbia to have full voting representation in Congress, many interest groups have formed, and others have been supportive of an initiative for change. The Coalition for DC Representation in Congress Education Fund, or DC Vote, is an interest group dedicated to a change in legislation that will provide Washingtonians with "the principles enumerated in the Constitution that guarantee democratic representation of all citizens." But how is DC Vote different from any other citizens' group fighting for voting rights in the District?

DC Vote is structured in a hierarchal manner, with a president, officers and a board of members. However, though there is a chain of authority within DC Vote, it does not deter input or active participation from every level of the organization. Within its mission statement, DC Vote solicits support from *anyone* who wishes to pursue the goal of attaining full voting rights through non-violent means. There are six factors which can provide the cohesion for an interest group: ethnicity, race, national origin, religion, policy issues or occupation/profession. In seeking such a diverse membership base, the focus of DC Vote is steadfast with the *full voting rights* issue, and the organization is not categorized beyond the mission. This inclusive approach mirrors the premise of representation for all people in Congress;

thus, DC Vote represents all citizens of Washington, DC and the policy issue of *full voting rights* is the cohesion for this interest group.

DC Vote is an institutional group that has a specific political function or goal. The membership is diverse in its makeup, but the political affiliations within that membership provide DC Vote with a strong voice in the Nation's Capital. It also provides the group with insight on how to generate capital. Mayor Anthony Williams pledged to raise one million dollars for the campaign to achieve full representation during his opening remarks at a welcome reception for DC Vote's executive director (dcvote.org/octnov.htm). DC Vote is an organization focused on educating the public about voting injustice and receives financial support from foundations, corporations and public donations in addition to charitable pledges previously mentioned (see Chapter 4 for details on fundraising by DC Vote).

Financial support provides DC Vote with the ability to campaign nationally for voting rights through mass media and, most importantly, on the Internet. Its Web site provides information about the organization, background on the issue, related activities and upcoming events, how to participate in and donate to the cause, and links to other sites referencing voting rights for Washington, DC. There is also a monthly newsletter that discusses the latest developments on the issue. In addition to the Web site, DC Vote has a fully staffed office on 1500 U Street, in Northwest Washington, DC where information is readily provided. DC Vote is not a loose band of District residents editorializing for congressional representation, but an organized coalition of United States citizens with an objective and political access.

> Not all citizens…are easily organized. Citizens with generally higher socioeconomic status-college educated, upper incomes, prestiguously employed, and high political efficacy-are associated with greater political participation. These individuals believe that the organization maximizes their opportunities to influence public policies most

salient to them. Those at the other end...tend to place
higher priority on their economic well-being (Mahood
2000:25).

The population in Washington, DC is majority African American,
with the average middle-income level of $30,680 per family (cbpp.org/pa-
dc.htm). A family consists of approximately three to four people. This
does not reflect the upper income stratum of the District, but it is a reflection of the majority of residents. On October 25, 2000, a welcome reception was held for the new executive director of DC Vote at Georgia
Brown's Restaurant in Washington, DC. Georgia Brown's is an expensive
restaurant and the requested minimum contribution for the event was
$100 per person, according to the invitation. The new executive director,
Amy Whitcomb Slemmer, is Caucasian. The president of DC Vote, Joe
Sternlieb, is Caucasian as well. The average African American family in
Washington, DC, logically, could not afford to attend the welcome cere-
mony. The majority of executive officials within the Coalition for DC
Representation in Congress Education Fund, or DC Vote, do not repre-
sent the racial majority of African American citizens in Washington, DC.
Do the previously mentioned realities contradict the mission of DC
Vote? No! They only illustrate the harsh realities of politics in America.
African Americans are less politically active, wield less political influence,
and hold fewer political offices than Caucasians. Although inactivity and
lack of influence can be partially attributed to the fact that African
Americans are a minority in the United States, there still is not a fair racial
representation in Congress, or any state legislature, based upon national
and state population statistics.

In contrast, DC Vote is an active proponent for change in the District,
change that will be inclusive of all citizens regardless of race, color or
creed. DC Vote has the organization, financial support and the political
affiliations to continue in its mission of attaining *full voting rights*, thus
making this organization a prospect for the future of Washington, DC.

The debate is far from over, but the issue is no longer local due to the work of interest groups like DC Vote.

Conclusion

On October 16, 2000, the United States Supreme Court declined to hear arguments in the *Alexander v Mineta* voting rights case. This case was brought forth in an effort to attain full representation in Congress on the grounds that representation is a constitutional right for the citizens of Washington, DC. This decision supports the outcome of the *Alexander v Daley* case, which determined that voting rights for District citizens must be achieved through congressional initiative and not by way of judicial intervention. Yet, Congress has allowed the citizens of Washington, DC to be disenfranchised for the last 200 years. Does this Supreme Court decision negate all prospects for voting rights in the District?

The Supreme Court decision did not negate any future prospects; it merely moved the debate back to Congress. Although voting rights have been up for debate for centuries, progress has been made. That progress has been most important in terms of awareness. The campaign for voting rights has spread nationally and various interest groups have formed to support full representation for the citizens of Washington, DC. Most United States citizens assume that the District is provided the same privileges afforded to them, so awareness is a key component for change.

According to information gathered by sociologist Mark Richards on "U.S. Public Opinion on Political Equality for Citizens of the District of Columbia," 72 percent of United States adults, 69 percent of college graduates who are registered to vote, state and local elected officials believe Washingtonians should have equal representation in Congress. His information also shows that 46 percent of United States adults and 55 percent of college graduates who are registered to vote are not even aware that Washingtonians do not have equal voting rights in Congress (dcwatch.com/Richards/000412.htm). Public support, on both the local and national level, is necessary to promote equality for District citizens and to ensure that the voting rights issue will reach the congressional floor once again.

Equal representation within the governing body is an unalienable right granted by the Constitution of the United States of America to all its citizens. However, Washington, DC is not a state within the United States of America, but a federal district where the federal government resides, independent of any one state (Harris 1995:223). Congress has an exclusive authority over Washington, DC, and voting rights is a step in the direction of statehood, which could possibly negate that congressional authority. Congress has not been open to relinquishing that authority, and the voting rights issue has become one of many other issues surrounding the status of Washington, DC. Voting rights in Washington, DC is an issue with no immediate resolution.

There have been many prospects for voting rights in Washington, DC, from statehood initiatives to citizen lawsuits; all of which have been unsuccessful in attaining full representation for Washingtonians. This chapter has outlined the various underlying factors such as race, political parties, and preeminent ideals that lay the foundation for the current state of political disempowerment in the District. Awareness has increased through interest groups such as DC Vote, yet there have been no substantial developments toward representation. Still, the struggle for equality continues; and where one prospect is rejected, another will be presented. The partisan breakdown of the federal government may suggest what the abrupt future holds regarding full representation in Congress, but only time will tell if Washington, DC can ever attain the voting rights outlined by the Constitution of the United States of America for its citizens. For more than 200 years, time has not had anything to say.

COMMENTARY

▼

DEMOCRACY ON TRIAL IN DC

Martin Thomas

July 26 (2000) was another sultry day in Washington and tourists crowded the museums, the monuments and the US Capitol. But visitors to the House of Representatives gallery that day got to see more than just relics of past struggles for freedom—they got to see democracy in action. I'm not talking about the normal House procedural motions and flabby rhetoric, but about the seven citizens of DC, who, denied democratic rights, stood up and voted the only way they could. Shouts of "Free DC" came from the seven of us, as we were pulled from the gallery by US Capitol police, handcuffed and arrested.

What made us feel so strongly that we had to jump up and take action in that way? Most DC residents, and more and more people nationwide, know that DC is denied any representation in Congress. What many don't know is that Congress, the same body that denies us a vote, also has final authority over DC's laws and budget.

On July 26 (2000), Congress was holding its annual debate on the DC budget, during which representatives from all across the land (with the exception of the District), decide how to spend our tax dollars. Each year our elected City Council passes a budget, which the mayor signs and that should be that. Instead our budget goes from House and Senate subcommittees, to full committees, and is then voted on by the Congress.

This is where Congresspeople cut money from programs they don't like and de-fund legislation. They have even overturned a citywide referendum by introducing amendments or "riders" to budget bills. Most of these attacks of late have reflected the right-wing ideology of the Republicans in charge of the committees, who view DC as a social laboratory for their policies.

So we are hit with a double whammy. First we are denied the rights enjoyed by all US citizens to have voting representation in the House and Senate. And second, we lack authority over our laws and budget. While, on philosophical grounds, we are outraged by this hijacking of democracy, we know that many of the congressional changes to our budget literally mean life or death for District residents. In the amendments this year, we lost our right to decide policies on needle exchange to reduce HIV transmission and medical marijuana for cancer and AIDS patients. In addition, we suffered cuts in funding for public transportation and are prohibited from spending funds to redress our lack of democracy in the courts and with our "Shadow" congressional delegation.

The struggle for DC democracy is decades long. Congressional action and even a constitutional amendment have failed. Two lawsuits, one seeking voting representation and one seeking full democracy, including budgetary and legislative autonomy, will be heard by the Supreme Court soon. As the procedural avenues to democracy close one by one, the seven of us took direct action, as many others in this civil rights struggle have before.

The "Democracy 7," Steve Donkin, Debby Hanrahan, Bette Hoover, Queen Mother ShemYah, Tanya Snyder, Karen Szulgit and I, are charged with disruption of Congress and face fines of up to $500 each and/or six months in prison if convicted. Prosecutors from the US Attorney's office have entered a motion to limit political speech during the trial.

What can you do to fight for DC democracy?

(1) Come to a rally for DC Democracy on September

29 (2000) before the "Democracy 7" trial at DC Superior Court (500 Indiana Avenue, NC, Judiciary Square metro). The rally begins at 8:00 a.m. and the trial starts at 9:00 a.m.

(2) Join the Stand Up for Democracy Coalition. This multi-partisan, diverse group has been on the front lines of the DC democracy struggle for years. We need your help to build it into a potent political force. Call (202)232-2500 or see http://www.standup for democracy.org for more information.

From the House gallery to the courts, join us in standing up for democracy and making the call for a "Free DC" loud and clear.

From *The Eagle*, September 25, 2000:A5. Reprinted with permission of the author.

COMMENTARY

▼

DC: VOTELESS, BUT NOT POWERLESS

Mark Plotkin

How long are we going to take it? How long are we in the District of Columbia going to quietly accept our second-class status and be, oh, so grateful to receive the crumbs of democracy?

The behavioral mode of this town is to at all times act appropriately. It's not considered good form to cause a fuss. So what if we, as residents of the Nation's capital, have no voting representation in our national legislature? We've learned to adapt to and accommodate this minor slight.

Some even think we should be grateful for what we have. According to former speaker of the House and self-professed American historian Newt Gingrich, we in the District "should be happy—we have more freedom than anyone in Cuba."

We have collectively conditioned ourselves to take the insult. A poll has shown that 60 percent of the country's college graduates don't even know we are denied full voting representation in both the House and Senate. But we remain discreetly quiet about our plight.

A presidential campaign is the perfect place and the ideal time to raise this subject. The dirty little secret about our democracy should be a campaign issue, but it's never raised. Even our supposed friends don't dare bring it up.

Al Gore is on record for full voting representation for the District. Even better, he was an original cosponsor of the DC statehood bill. But he has obviously made the political judgment that he need not mention our unfortunate situation this year (2000). He knows our three electoral votes are in the bag.

The 23rd Amendment permitted us for the very first time to vote for president. Since 1964, the District has voted for the Democratic presidential candidate every time. In fact, no state has ever approached the margins we deliver for the Democratic Party standard-bearer. Because we are such a political certainty, the head of the ticket feels no obligation or responsibility to pay us any attention.

When I asked Gore campaign manager Donna Brazile about mentioning our voteless status in Gore's acceptance speech at the Democratic Convention in Los Angeles, she said they might try to "slip it in." The vice president did not include it in his speech.

The District of Columbia is just not on the political radar screen. We have allowed ourselves to be taken for granted. It's time to put an end to this abusive relationship—one in which we automatically cast our votes for the Democratic candidate and ask absolutely nothing in return.

I'm not suggesting a vote for George W. Bush, who has stated unequivocally that he favors no voting representation for the District in either house. But what will make Al Gore take notice and pay more than lip service to the issue is for the three DC presidential electors to make a pledge—now—to cast not a ballot for Gore but instead a blank ballot.

David Scott, a longtime listener to WAMU (American University Radio), wrote to me and suggested the blank-ballot approach. His suggested act of political disobedience would alert the rest of the country that our polite and accommodating ways are officially over.

No longer are we to be considered a political eunuch, a sure thing. No longer are we to be overlooked, ignored and forgotten.

The local Democratic Party, which selects the three presidential electors, should make it clear right now that it will not select any individual who does not pledge to cast a blank ballot. I know this proposal will be considered reckless and even counterproductive, but I have to ask: What have we got by acting in the usual polite manner? It's time that we act clearly and dramatically to bring attention to this city's situation.

In the tightest and closest presidential race in 40 years, the District of Columbia needs to assert itself and play a role. Let us not continue to diminish ourselves in the American political universe. Our three electoral votes give us standing and political currency. It's time to use them.

From *The Washington Post*, Wednesday, Ocrober 18, 2000:A33. Reprinted with permission of the author.

Postscript

When the Washington, DC Electors met on December 18, 2000, William Simons and Nadine Winter voted for Al Gore while Barbara Lett-Simmons turned in a blank ballot. Before that, there had been just nine instances in United States Electoral College history of "faithless electors" who had broken party ranks.

During a telephone interview conducted by the editor of this book (Abdul Karim Bangura) with Winter on January 2, 2001, she stated that Mark Plotkin contacted all three of them (i.e. Electors) on several occasions urging them to turn in blank ballots. Thus, Winter suggested that Lett-Simmons must have been influenced by Plotkin. Attempts by the editor to contact Lett-Simmons were unsuccessful, and a voice-mail message was never returned.

COMMENTARY

▼

DC COUNTS!

John-John Williams IV and Karen Richards

Monday, amid the sweet sounds of Go-Go legend Chuck Brown and dark skies, distraught residents assembled and shredded, ripped and destroyed copies of their federal tax forms in protest. Protesters held up signs and passed out flyers in the latest chapter of the District's 200-year "taxation without representation" saga.

The protest, which was organized by DC Vote, took place at Upper Senate Park–directly across the street from the US Capitol.

DC Vote is a nonprofit organization of more than 40 local and national groups working to educate Congress and the American people about the need for full voting representation in the House of Representatives and the Senate through a process that reflects the will of the citizens.

The District of Columbia has no representation in the US Senate and one non-voting member in the House of Representatives. Amy Whitcomb

Slemmer, executive director for DC Vote, said the purpose of the protest was to alert others about this issue.

"Our goal is to raise a cry loud enough to be heard around the globe and finally heeded by the US Congress, which holds our fate in their hands," Slemmer said. "Today's protest provides an opportunity for citizens from all walks of life to express their discontent about taxation without representation in Washington, DC."

The cloudy skies did not deter the hundreds of Washingtonians, of different backgrounds, from making their voices heard.

Banneker High School junior Esther Samaria was on hand to give her unique perspective.

"I am here to speak to the youth," said the member of the Community Alliance of Youth Action. "If adults cannot vote then we cannot vote. The youth should be concerned about this."

Paul Strauss, the shadow senator for Washington, DC, expressed his displeasure with the state of the District.

"DC voters can vote for me but I can't vote for them," Strauss said. "It is unjust, unfair and inappropriate."

Kevin Moore, who was wearing a bright red "taxation without representation: shirt, was one of the organizers of the protest. He said this was the first step to bring attention to their cause.

"On tax day we are protesting to bring light to the fact that DC has the highest tax bill second to Connecticut," Moore said. "Kids can fight in war but cannot make a decision on whether to go to war. The only people who are disenfranchised other than DC citizens are children and convicted felons. We need to have a voice in Congress."

Keynote speaker Roger Wilkins, a professor at George Mason University and a member of DC's Board of Education, told the protesters that the day's event was a step in the right direction.

"The campaign to achieve representation in Congress for the citizens of DC is at the heart of any effort to fulfill America's promise of equal opportunity for all citizens," Wilkins said. "Today we move one important step closer to extending the full voting franchise to the citizens of the District of Columbia and completing the next phase of our nation's great civil rights movement."

The Monday protest was the latest in a long line of news-making events for the issue of full voting rights.

In October, Delegate Eleanor Holmes Norton gave a stirring speech about District representation when presidential candidate Al Gore came to Howard University during a rally.

In November, Mayor Anthony Williams pledged to raise $1 million for the campaign to achieve ful representation in Congress for the citizens of the District during a DC Vote reception.

At the time there was a successful campaign to change the slogan of District licence plates to: "Taxation Without Representation."

"This is an advertisement for the 25 million people that visit the District every year—we want everyone to know our situation," Williams said.

While citizens shredded their tax forms to let the world know about the District's plight, Strauss vowed that this wouldn't be the end.

"We are not giving up," he said. "We are going to the House of Representatives, Senate, and the people. This must end."

From the *Community News*, April 19, 2001:1. Reprinted with permission of the authors.

COMMENTARY

▼

VOTING RIGHTS:
BACK TO CONGRESS

The Washington Post

THE SUPREME Court's rejection of the District's claim to have a constitutional right to congressional voting representation is a disappointment but not a surprise. From the start, backers of the effort knew they had to clear a high legal bar. They were right, however, to appeal an earlier three judge panel's 2 to 1 vote against the District. The action now reverts to Congress, which has the poqwer to remedy an injustice that has been imposed on District residents since 1800.

The high court's decision, while closing the judiciary's doors to the District's arguments, does not reduce the moral case for voting rights. It is, pure and simple, wrong to deny District residents the right to send representatives to Congress who can vote on taxes or help decide questions of war and peace while at the same time expecting city residents to bear the

full burden of citizenship, including the obligation to pay billions in federal taxes and to fight and die for their country. It is wrong to apply the
principle of one person, one vote to all Americans except convicted felons
and District residents. It is wrong to deny residents of the nation's capital
the full political participation that is their due.

Winning support for full representation in the House and Senate is a
long shot, given the current political composition of Congress. But that is
no reason for advocates to cease working on legislative solutions to end the
disenfranchisement of District voters. January (2001) will usher in a new
Congress—and with it a new opportunity for the District to plead a cause
that is powerful, rooted in principle and unassailable.

From *The Washington Post*, Wednesday, October 18, 2000:A32. Reprinted
with permission of the author.

COMMENTARY

▼

TAXED, BUT NOT REPRESENTED

Julianne Malveaux

Patriots tossed tea into the Boston Harbor 227 years ago to protest taxation without representation. Now, thanks to a Supreme Court decision this week that rejected voting rights for residents of the District of Columbia, more than a half-million tax-paying citizens share a mantra with those Boston patriots.

Democrat Eleanor Holmes Norton, the District's delegate to the House, can vote in committee, but not on the House floor like a "real" representative. DC residents pay federal taxes and must obey federal laws, but can't hold Congress accountable for either if no one casts a ballot on their behalf during House and Senate votes.

When Americans descend on DC to lobby for, say, fair treatment of developing nations, it is ironic that they come to a District with fewer voting rights than those of some of those countries. How do people get so passionate about world democracy while remaining indifferent to the disenfranchisement of fellow citizens? DC radio commentator Mark Plotkin, a passionate voting rights advocate, says 60% of college graduates don't know that District residents have no vote in Congress. Bur does disenfranchisement also possibly have to do with the fact that DC is majority African-American and heavily Democratic?

Congress easily could redress this. That, however, would require it to put principle over politics, which isn't likely if Republicans continue to dominate it. Nor is it a given if Democrats take over; the party's platform supports DC voting rights, but the issue received scant mention at this summer's convention.

Norton says she will submit legislation authorizing full congressional representation for the District when the new Congress starts in January. But members of Congress won't support voting rights for DC unless their constituents pressure them to do so. If those who talk about fairness for developing countries would put pen on paper on behalf of the District, maybe a half-million Americans wouldn't be as disenfranchised as the folks whose taxation without representation sparked the war that created our country.

From the *USA Today*, Friday, October 20, 2000:17A. Reprinted with permission of the author.

BIBLIOGRAPHY

▼

Abbott, Carl. 1999. *Political Terrain: Washington, DC, from Tidewater Town to Global Metropolis*. Chapel Hill, North Carolina: University of North Carolina Press.

Almond, Gabriel A. 1958. A comparative study of interest groups and the political process. *American Political Science Review* 52, 1 (March).

Apidta, Tingba. 1998. *The Hidden History of Washington, DC*. Roxbury, Massachusetts: The Reclamation Project.

Austin-Smith, David. 1995. Campaign contributions and access. *American Political Science Review* 89, 3 (September).

Baker, Frederic. 1931. *The Erection of the White House*. Washington, DC: Records of the Columbia Historical Society.

Barker, Lucius J. et al. 1999. *African Americans and the American Political System*, 4th ed. Upper Saddle River, New Jersey: Prentice Hall Press.

Bauer, D. 1999. *Successful Grantseeking Techniques for Obtaining Public and Private Grants*. Phoenix, Arizona: Onyx Press.

Bentley, Arthur. 1908. *The Process of Government*. Evanston, Illinois: Principal Press.

Berman, L. and B. Murphy. 1999. *Approaching Democracy*. Upper Saddle River, New Jersey: Prentice Hall.

Berry, Jeffrey M. 1989. *The Interest Group Society*. Glenview, Illinois: Scott, Foresman and Company.

Best, Judith. 1984. *National Representation for the District of Columbia*. Frederick, MD: University Publications.

Bryan, Wihelmus B. 1916. *A History of the National Capital: From its Foundation through the Period of the Adoption of the Organic Act*. New York, New York: Macmillan Publishing Company.

Burns, J., J. Peltason, T. Cronin and D. Magleby. 1997. *Government by the People*. River, New Jersey: Simon and Schuster.

Caldeira, Gregory A. and J. Wright. 1988. Organized interests and agenda setting in the US Supreme Court. *American Political Science Review* 82, 4 (December).

Chong, Dennis. 1991. *Collective Action and the Civil Rights Movement*. Chicago, Illinois: The University of Chicago Press.

Cooper, Timothy. 1996. Abolish DC. *The New Republic* December 5.

Craig, Lois. 1978. *The Federal Presence: Architecture, Politics, and Symbols in United States Government Buildings*. Cambridge, Massachusetts: Massachusetts Institute of Technology Press.

Daly, J. and J. Keen. 1997. Soft money of parties tripled, since 1992. *Press Release* (February 17). Washington, DC: Center for Responsive Politics.

DC Vote Newsletter. September 2000.

DC Vote Newsletter. April 2000.

Deakin, James. 1966. *The Lobbyists*. Washington, DC: Public Affairs Press.

Denzau, Arthur T. and M. Munger. 1986. How organized interests get represented. *American Political Science Review* 80, 1 (March).

Dillon, Mary Earhart. 1942. Pressure groups. *American Political Science Review* 36, 3 (June).

District of Columbia. 1985. Statehood hearings. Washington, DC: House of Representatives.

Dye, Thomas. 2000. *Politics in States and Communities*. Upper Saddle River, New Jersey: Prentice Hall.

Edles, P. 1993. *Fundraising: Hands on Tactics for Nonprofit Groups*. New York, New York: McGraw-Hill.

Elliot, Jeffrey M. 1986. *Black Voices in American Politics*. San Diego, California: Harcourt Brace Jovanovich, Publishers.

Engelman, Robert. 1986. Clipping from the Historical Society of Washington, DC. *The Washington Post Magazine* (July 13).

Freedman, H. and K. Feldman. 1998. *The Business of Special Events: Fundraising Strategies for Changing Times*. Sarasota, Florida: Pineapple.

Furer, Howard B., ed. 1975. *Washington: A Chronological and Documentary History 1790-1970*. Oceana Publications, Inc.

Georgetown Public Policy Institute. 1996. *The District of Columbia as a National Capital and the District of Columbia as a Place to Live: A History of Local Governance to Present Day*. Washington, DC: Georgetown Public Policy Institute.

Gillettee, Howard. 1995. *Between Justice and Beauty: Race, Planning, and the Failure of Urban Policy in Washington, DC*. Baltimore, Maryland: Johns Hopkins University Press.

Godwin, K. 1998. *One Billion Dollars of Influence: The Direct Marketing of Politics*. New York, New York: Chatham House.

Graham, Wilson. 1990. *Interest Groups*. Oxford, England: Basil Blackwell Publishers.

Green, Constance McLaughlin. 1967. *The Secret City: A History of Race Relations in the Nation's Capital*. Princeton, New Jersey: Princeton University Press.

Green, Constance McLaughlin. 1962-63. *Washington: Capital City*. Princeton, New Jersey: Princeton University Press.

Gutheim, Frederick A. 1976. *The Federal City: Plans and Realities.* Washington, DC: Smithsonian Institution Press. W. W. Norton and Company.

Harris, Charles Wesley. 1995. *Congress and the Governance of the Nation's Capital: The Conflict of Federal and Local Interests.* Washington, DC: Georgetown University Press.

Heckathorn, Douglass. 1996. The dynamics and dilemmas of collective action. *American Sociological Review* 61:250-277.

Henry, Shannon. 1999. DC region leads nation in net access. *The Washington Post* (October 17).

Horton, Lois Elaine. 1977. The development of federal social policy for Blacks in Washington, DC after emancipation. Ph.D. Dissertation, Brandeis University.

Hrebenar, Ronald J. and Ruth K. Scott. 1968 & 1990. *Interest Group Politics in America,* 1st & 2nd eds. Englewood Cliffs, New Jersey: Prentice Hall.

http://home.dn.net/~schaefer/fdp.html

http://www.advocacy.com/guidelines.html

http://www.cbpp.org/pa-dc.htm

http://www.dcchamber.gov

http://www.dcvote.org

http://www.dcwatch.com/Richards/000412.htm

http://www.folner.org/grantmaker

http://www.house.gov/Norton/pr00329.htm

http://www.jirs.org/jir/8cOnjy

http://www.jirs.org/jirs/8cOnyry.htm

http://www.meyerfoundation.org/info

http://www.narpac.org/ITXGU6A.HTM

http://www.tidesfoundation.org/aboutus.cfm

http://xroads.virginia.edu/~CAP/ANACOSTIA/early.html

Hughes, Jonathan. 1976. *Social Control in the Colonial Economy*. Charlottesville, Virginia: University Press of Virginia.

Jackson, Brooks. 1990. *Honest Graft: Big Money and the American Political Process*. Washington, DC: Farragut Publishing Company.

Jacob, Kathryn A. 1995. *Capital Elites: High Society in Washington, DC after the Civil war*. Washington, DC: Smithsonian Institution Press.

Janda, Kenneth et al. 1995. *The Challenge of Democracy*, 4th ed. Boston, Massachusetts: Houghton Mifflin Company.

Jet Magazine. July 22, 1996.

Johnson, Otto, ed. 1997. *Information Please Almanac* 50th Anniversary Edition. Boston, Massachusetts: Houghton Mifflin Company.

Latham, Earl. 1952. The group basis of politics: Notes for a theory. *American Political Science Review* 46, 2:376-397.

Lewis, David L. 1976. *District of Columbia: A Bicentennial History*. New York, New York: W. W. Norton and Company, Incorporated.

Lowi, Theodore. 1979. *The End of Liberalism: Ideology, Policy, and the Crisis of Public Authority*. New York, New York: Norton Publishers.

Mahood, H. R. 1990 & 2000. *Interest Groups in American National Politics: An Overview*, 1st & 2nd eds. Upper Saddle River, New Jersey: Prentice Hall.

McGuire, Kevin J. and G. Caldeira. 1993. Lawyers, organized interests, and the law of obscenity: Agenda setting in the Supreme Court. *American Political Science Review* 87, 3 (September).

Meade, Robert Douthat. 1969. *Patrick Henry: Practical Revolutionary*. Philadelphia, Pennsylvania: J. B. Lippincott Press.

National Capital Planning Commission. 1929-2000. *Annual Reports*. Washington, DC: Government Printing Office.

Nicolay, Helen. 1924. *Our capital on the Potomac*. New York, New York: Alfred A. Knopf.

Olson, Mancur. 1965. *The Logic of Collective Action: Public Goods and the Theory of Groups.* Cambridge, Massachusetts: Harvard University Press.

Ornstein, Norman J. and Shirley Elder. 1978. *Interest Groups, Lobbying and Policymaking.* Washington, DC: Congressional Quarterly Press.

Pateman, Carole. 1970. *Participation and Democratic Theory.* Cambridge, England: Cambridge University Press.

Peterson, Mark A. 1992. The presidency and organized interests: White House patterns of interest group liaison. *American Political Science Review* 86, 3 (September).

Rosenthal, Alan. 1993. *The Third House: Lobbying and Lobbyists in the States.* Washington, DC: Congressional Quarterly, Inc.

Rothenberg, L. 1992. *Linking Citizens to Government: Interest Group Politics at Common Cause.* New York, New York: Cambridge University Press.

Rounds, Elizabeth. n.d. *Lost Arrows: The Story of the Indians in the District of Columbia,* [juvenile] 970.4R859 wash/Ref.

Salisbury, Robert. 1970. *Interest Group Politics in America.* New York, New York: Harper & Row Publishers.

Schattschneider, E. E. 1972. *Party Government.* New York, New York: Farar and Rinehart.

Schattschneider, E. E. 1981. *Semi-Sovereign People.* New York, New York: Holt, Rinehart & Winston.

Smith, Richard A. Advocacy, interpretation and influence in the US Congress. *American Political Science Review* 78, 1 (March).

Stern, Robert A. M. 1991. A temenos for democracy: The Mall in Washington and its influences. In National Gallery of Art, ed. *The Mall in Washington, 1791-1991.* Washington, DC: National Gallery of Art Publications.

Tremain, Mary. 1969. *Slavery in the District of Columbia* New York, New York: Negro Universities Press.

Truman, David B. 1951 & 1971. *The Governmental Process*, 1st and 2nd eds. New York, New York: Alfred A. Knopf.

United States Congress. 1990. *Governance of the Nation's Capital: A Summary of the Forms and Powers of Local Government for the District of Columbia, 1790-1973* (House Committee on the District of Columbia, 101st. Congress, 2nd Session). Washington, DC: United States Government Printing Office.

Weller, Charles F. 1908. Neglected neighborhoods. In *The Presidents' Home Commission*. In David L. Lewis, ed. 1976. *District of Columbia: A Bicentennial History*. New York, New York: W. W. Norton and Company, Incorporated.

Weller, Charles F. 1909. *Neglected Neighbors: Stories of Life in the Alleys, Tenements, and Shanties of the National capital.* Philadelphia, Pennsylvania: J. C. Winston.

Whipple, Paul W. 1985. Ten myths of DC statehood (unpublished paper). Washington, DC: Reference Library.

Whipple, Paul W. 1984. Governing the Nation's Capital: Is statehood the answer? (Draft testimony). Washington, DC: Reference Library.

Wilson, T. 1993. *American Government: Institutions and Policies*. Boston, Massachusetts: Heath and Company.

Wilson, William H. 1989. *The City Beautiful Movement*. Baltimore, Maryland: Johns Hopkins University Press.

Wolpe, Bruce and Bertram Levine. 1996. *Lobbying Congress: How the System Works*. Washington, DC: Congressional Quarterly, Incorporated.

World Book Encyclopedia. 1976. Chicago, Illinois: Field Enterprises Educational Corporation.

Wright, John R. 1985. PACs, contributions, and roll calls: An organizational perspective. *American Political Science Review* 79, 2 (June).

Zeigler, Hamon L. and G. Wayne Peak. 1972. *Interest Groups in American Politics*, 2nd ed. Englewood Cliffs, New Jersey: Prentice Hall.

ABOUT THE CONTRIBUTORS

▼

Abdul Karim Bangura is a professor of International Relations and a researcher-in-residence at the Center for Global Peace in the School of International Service at American University, and Director of The African Institution in Washington, DC. He holds Ph.D. degrees in Political Science, Policy Sciences (concentration in Development Economics), Linguistics, and Computer Science.

Kathy Booh is a graduate student in Political Science, specializing in International Relations and American Government and Politics, at Howard University.

Ray M. Crawford, Jr. is a graduate student in Political Science, specializing in American Government and Politics and Public Administration, at Howard University. He also is affiliated with the United States Federal Emergency Management Agency.

Julianne Malveaux is syndicated columnist whose weekly column has appeared nationally in some 20 newspapers since 1990. Malveaux is a radio talk show host and has appeared on many television talk shows. She has taught economics, public policy, and African American studies, most recently at the University of California, Berkeley. She received her Ph.D. in Economics from the Massachusetts Institute of Technology.

Lisa Nicole Nealy is a doctoral candidate in Political Science, specializing in American Government and Politics and Black Politics, at Howard University. She also is a Teaching Fellow and a published author.

Patrick D. Nemons is a graduate student in Political Science, specializing in Public Administration and American Government and Politics, at Howard University. He also is the President and Chief Executive Officer of Top of The World Productions and works for the United States Department of Transportation Office of the Inspector General.

Mark Plotkin is a local political commentator for the American University WAMU-Radio in Washington, DC.

Karen Richards writes for the *Community News*, a newspaper in Washington, DC.

Carol J. Roberts is a graduate student in Political Science, specializing in American Government and Politics and Public Administration, at Howard University.

Martin Thomas is the Washington, DC Statehood Green Party's candidate for Shadow United States Representative.

Damon Waters received his M.A. in Political Science degree, specializing in American Government and Politics and Black Politics, this May from Howard University. He is a writer for the Alliances for Quality Education, Inc. He plans to begin work for a Ph.D. in Political Science and a JD in Civil Rights Law.

John-John Williams IV is tempo editor for the *Community News*, a newspaper in Washington, DC. He is also currently working at the *Chicago Tribune*.

The Washington Post is the major newspaper in Washington, DC.

ABOUT THE BOOK

▼

This book is an outgrowth of a special seminar on Pressure Groups conducted in the Department of Political Science at Howard University during the fall of 2000. The major focus of the seminar was on DC Vote. The chapters in this book are revised versions of the papers that were presented at the seminar. Since the chapters employ an interest-group perspective to investigate various aspects of DC Vote's efforts to influence decision-makers at all branches of government and throughout the United States, the book is a valuable tool for instructors and students in most areas of American Government and Politics, especially National Government, State and Local Government, Interest Group Politics, Public Administration, and Political Behavior.

ABOUT THE EDITOR

▼

Abdul Karim Bangura is a professor of International Relations and a researcher-in-residence at the Center for Global Peace in the School of International Service at American University, and the director of The African Institution in Washington, DC. Bangura holds Ph.D. degrees in Political Science, Development Economics, Linguistics, and Computer Science. He is the author of 19 books and more than 200 scholarly articles. He is the president-elect of the Association of Third World Studies and a member of many and hold offices in several other scholarly organizations. He is the editor-in-chief of two refereed journals—the *Journal of Research Methodology and African Studies* and the *African Journal of Languages and Linguistics*—and serves on the editorial boards of many others. He has won numerous teaching, research and community service awards. He also is fluent in about a dozen African and six European languages.